Lions Savage
1914 - 1918

**The War through the eyes of a Soldier in
"The Royal West Kent Regiment"**

Compiled by Ray Cantan

Registered with the IP Rights Office Copyright
Registration Service
Ref: 7563252700

PROLOGUE

Most of you will know what the title - "Lions Savaged by Donkeys" – means; however, in case there are some .readers who have not met the terms before I will give a brief explanation

The German frontline troops had a high respect for the British Tommy and nicknamed them collectively as the 'Lions'. This was because of their courage and tenacity. They had zero respect for the British Officers and, jokingly, nicknamed them the 'Donkeys'. The Germans, facing the British Regiments, couldn't believe what they were seeing at times. Thousands of brave men, emerging from the enemy trenches and then walking across No-Man's Land towards the German lines, in broad daylight, with huge packs on their backs, going to their inevitable deaths. Throughout the war, the British troops in the vanguard of the offensives followed the orders they were given, and there were no mutinies. Even though they knew that they would most likely lose their life as a result of, what they regarded as crazy instructions, they still kept going. This book is dedicated to the hundreds and thousands of 'Lions' who lost their lives and, more especially, to Sid Kemp, a Private in the Royal West Kent Regiment. He kept a diary and wrote down his experiences from the time he enlisted in August 1914 until he was invalided out in 1917. It is his story that is the basis of this book.

On April 16th, 1916 my own Grandfather, Lieutenant Colonel H T Cantan, was killed in the trenches close to Arras in Northern France. He was a professional soldier aged forty-seven and was the Commanding Officer of the 1st Battalion the Duke of Cornwall's Light Infantry

(DCLI) at the time of his death. On the day that he was killed, he was due to leave the front and return to England as he was to be made up to be a Brigadier and his next step was to attend Staff College.

He had joined the Army as a Private when he was sixteen and had been in the Army all his life. An excellent sportsman, he had represented the DCLI at many inter-regimental tournaments, home and abroad. He joined as a Private and had been made up to be an officer in the early 1990's which was a very rare event in the Victorian Army. He married my Grandmother in Dublin near the end of the previous century having met her while he was stationed at the Curragh Camp in Ireland.

Being originally a 'Ranker', if his troops suffered, he suffered. He was very popular amongst his men, and his desire to say goodbye to the troops under his command led to his death. Before he left the battlefield to get his transport back to England and safety, he went up to the front line to see them one more time. He reckoned that there was no danger as the Arras Battlefield was quiet at the time. His luck was up, and while he was in the front line trench, a German Whizz Bang mortar bomb came over and killed him.

He had written to my Grandmother a few days previously and told her that he was leaving for England on April 15th. She naturally assumed when she got up on April 16th that he would be back in England by then and she started to relax knowing that he was at last safe. When the telegram arrived informing her of his death, she was shattered, and never really recovered until her death in 1952, thirty-six years later.

In my formative years, I spent a lot of time at my Grandmothers, and, as a child, I remember playing games using his military memorabilia. When I asked my Mother where it came from, I was told that my Grandfather had left it there when he went off to war in 1914, but that he had never returned as he had been killed in that war. I wasn't told any of the details or even where he was buried. As far as I am aware, my Grandmother never visited his grave at Arras, Northern France, but she may have in the early years after the First World War. It was a long way to travel from Tullow, in Ireland, where she lived, to the North of France as it meant going the whole way across England to London, and then going from there across the Channel to France. There were no cheap flights in those days!

I never had the time or inclination to go and find where he was buried, until I retired to Kent in 2014. I made a big effort to travel to his grave on the centenary of his death in 1916. In fact, I went at the end of November 2015, and I placed a wreath, emblazoned with the DCLI crest, on his grave. It was a very moving moment for me, and I immediately felt a strong bond with the Grandfather who had lain in the Faubourg-d'Amiens Cemetery at Arras for close on one hundred years. I felt that, as a family, we had ignored the fact that he had existed and given his life for what he believed in. I remember feeling very relieved that his grave was in a cemetery that was in a bustling town and not stuck out in some remote field as a lot of the war graves were. I know that it doesn't make sense, but I felt that he wouldn't have felt lonely.

I have returned to pay homage at his grave since that first time and the last time I was there I had my lunch beside his headstone. When I returned home, I told my friends in the Western Front Association that I had lunch with my Grandfather! He has a very nice position in the Cemetery as he was one of the first buried there. The Cemetery was opened on April 8^{th,} 1916, and he was killed on the 16th.

While I was visiting the Cemetery, I looked around at the headstones of those who have been resting alongside him for the past hundred years. I was amazed to see how young a lot of the soldiers were when they met their end. In fact, I was shocked by what I was reading. My Grandfather was a professional soldier and had served in the Second Boer War and other parts of the world. As part of his profession, he knew that there was a risk he might get killed, and I, as a relative can understand and accept his death in the grand scheme of things. It was his job and what he signed up for. All the teenagers, and there were a lot of them, were on a big adventure especially the ones who volunteered for Kitchener's Army. Their Mothers would have expected the Generals to have looked after their sons and not to have fed them to the German Machine Guns chasing unobtainable and unrealistic objectives.

While visiting one of the memorials on the battlefield at Mametz, I found the name of another of my relatives which surprised me as I hadn't heard of any other members of my family having being killed in the First World War. He was killed in 1918 at the age of eighteen which meant that he must have enlisted at the age of sixteen as he signed on in 1916.

The last time I was at my Grandfather's grave, in November 1916, I made a pledge to him that I would try and reconcile, in my own mind, whether the enormous number of deaths were unavoidable or whether the Generals must be apportioned some or all of the blame. I am not a Military Strategist and what I am about to write, is not examining or criticising the strategy that the Generals used. Rather, I want to look at whether the basics of common-sense were followed, and before you get on your high horse, I know that common-sense in 1914 is not the same as common-sense in 2016.

For example, I fail to see how anybody in their right mind could possibly believe that the cavalry regiments were going to make the big breakthrough on the Western Front. Horses against Machine Guns seems to me to be an unequal match, yet, Field Marshal Haig latterly and General French before him, both believed that the cavalry would be the means that they would win the war. Interestingly enough they both came from Cavalry Regiments, which, before 1914, were the elite regiments of the British Army. The amount of resources that were required to sustain the Cavalry Regiments; the horses themselves and the food they consumed to name but two, was huge. All this cost and effort led to zero contribution to the effectiveness of the BEF. Doesn't make sense, does it?

At the start of this year, 2017, a friend of mine was going through her late husband's effects, and she came across a manuscript written by a man called Sid Kemp. He enlisted as a Private in the Royal West Kent Regiment in August 1914. Not having any need for the document she asked me if I would like it. His account of the day to day activities of an enlisted man from the time he signed up at the end of August 1914, until he was invalided out in 1917, is just what I needed for my analysis. I have used his observations to help me understand what was going on and whether things could have been done differently, with fewer losses. I can assure you that I have not altered his manuscript in any way.

He enlisted in the 6th Service Battalion of 'The Queen's Own' Royal West Kent Regiment. He states that his story is written in Remembrance of my friends who served in The West Kents and never returned to the England that they loved. I also want to dedicate the additional 'Reflections' that I have written to their memory and his. I have enquired around and as far as I can establish his account has never been published.

The book is mainly about his experiences; however, I have inserted some Reflections where I feel they are appropriate. I hope that you can use what has been written to arrive at your own conclusions.

Chapter 1

The year 1914 will not be remembered in history for the weather or who won the FA Cup final played at the Crystal Palace in April, but for the start of the most terrible war that the world had ever seen. I was working, as I had been for the past two and a half years, at Oxon Hoath, Hadlow, as a gardener. Born in Kent in 1891 I reached the age of twenty-three years on my Birthday, April 5th, 1914. Top of my list of worries was the fact that I was getting old and still had not met the girl who I wished to marry and spend my life with. Was there something wrong with me?

On April 13th, which was Easter Monday, I met Ethel Ashdown for the first time and, amazingly, I know that we both loved each other from that first meeting. Ethel was nineteen years of age, but Oh wasn't she lovely in both looks and personality.

1914 had started off with major troubles again occurring in Ireland, which, at the time, was one country. There was talk of a revolt of the army, currently under the Generalship of John French, at the Curragh Camp which was situated about thirty miles south of Dublin.

It all had to do with the order issued to the Officers of the troops based in the Curragh that if there was a military revolt in the Northern part of Ireland, the British Army would have to fire on other British countrymen to maintain Law and Order. They refused to accept that they might have to shoot their own countrymen even if they were Northern Irish. It was a very tense situation, and anything could have happened. However, the crisis with Germany and the threat of war seemed to push that problem down the ladder of importance.

At that time we were governed by a Liberal Government, under Prime Minister Herbert Asquith. His nickname was "Mr Wait and See" so from the nickname you can see that he wasn't known for taking quick decisions. The Foreign Secretary was Sir Edward Grey, with Mr Lloyd George as Chancellor and Winston Churchill as First Lord of the Admiralty. This Liberal Government was one of a succession of Liberal Governments which were first elected in January 1906 with an overwhelming majority over the Conservative party. They had held office for the previous eleven years without a break.

One of the primary objectives of the Liberal Government was to improve conditions for the lower paid workers, and it was because of this that they had been elected. They passed the Old-Age Pension Act in 1908 which gave five shillings per week to the over seventy age group. It was only paid provided the pensioner didn't have too much money in their bank account. It was basically a means test which was open to abuse. Next, Lloyd George, in 1912, introduced the nine pence for four pence scheme which was the introduction of the Health Service. Fourpence was stopped from a workers wages, then, when the employee went sick, the four pence would be increased by three pence from the employer and two pence from the state. A lot of the effort and brain power of the Government went into these types of improvements during the years 1907 to 1912.

Both of these Liberal measures have stood the test of time, and both were a boon to people who, when they were ill or attained the age of seventy, were now sure of a small wage. Up to then old folk, who were unable to work, were dependent on their children and charity. In the local community, folk did their best to help the old ones.

At that time, sugar could be bought for twopence per lb; beer cost two pence to three pence per pint, loose tobacco was three pence, and fags were five for a penny. If we earned ten shillings or more, we were usually paid in gold; a half-sovereign, with silver making up the rest of what we were due. Those earning a wage of £1 almost always received a Gold Sovereign. Britain at that time was wealthy and was overstocked, as it is now, with too many workers. Unemployment was a feature then as it is now.

The Summer of 1914 was a lovely one, not as nice as the Summer of 1911, the year of the coronation of King George V and Queen Mary, but it was fine enough to be enjoyable.

I must retrace my steps here and tell you about the events surrounding King Edward VII, the previous King. He came to the throne in 1901 and was crowned King of England in August 1902. The original coronation date was set for the 26th. June but that had to be postponed after he became ill with Appendicitis two days before the original June date.

His chief concern, after he became King, was to establish better relations with France. For obvious reasons, the French had hated the British since the defeat of Napoleon at Waterloo in 1815. Also, Britain had not gone to the aid of France in the Franco-Prussian war of 1870.

The King set in motion the process to draw up a treaty which committed Britain to go to the aid of France if Germany should invade them as they had done in 1870. The treaty was called the Entente Cordiale. Britain and France signed up to go to each other's aid if either country was attacked by Germany. King Edward VII did not trust his cousin Kaiser Wilhelm II of Germany because the Kaiser claimed that he had a right to the throne of England. His mother was Queen Victoria's eldest daughter, older than Edward, who, of course, had been crowned King.

As a result of his war mongering nature and his desire to be King of England, the Kaiser decided to build a large fleet of battleships so Germany could rule the oceans should war come about. At that time Germany had very few oversea possessions so their navy would only have to operate in the North Sea and the Channel. In 1905, they started to construct battleships that were heavily armour-plated and with massive guns. All these large battleships would have to do in a war was cross the North Sea and attack England, so they didn't need speed or agility, all they required was massive firepower. The British Admiralty responded to this threat by ordering the Dreadnought class battleship to be built. As well as patrolling the Empire, these ships would have to see off the threat of the German battleships. They would need speed as well as guns to match the German ones. They sacrificed heavy armour to make the ships lighter giving them better speed. The race was on, and the shipyards across Britain were flat out constructing Dreadnoughts; they had to keep pace with the German building programme.

Still, the populace was not alarmed as the threat to Great Britain wasn't seen as being real. No one worried too much, and life just went on. If you had a job, you were able to get by. No working people in those days could save money; the only saving most people had was a two or three penny policy with the Prudential to ensure that when they died, they could be buried properly. That seemed to be a major concern for most people over the age of forty. People were content even though they were just surviving. A few had a gramophone at home; you were able to buy records at sixpence each, and they gave enjoyment. There was no wireless yet, although Marconi was beginning to beam signals across the Atlantic, but, at that time, it was the limit of wireless signal technology.

There were a few small aircraft which could be spotted now and again. Any plane was still a great novelty and caused a stir when one appeared. I saw my first flying machine in June 1911 when I was twenty years of age. I actually touched one in Mote Park, Maidstone. I went to see Kent play cricket at the County Ground, based in the Park. This plane landed behind the where the people were watching the match. Being pretty agile, I was the first one out of my seat on the rows of raised planks around the ground, and I was able to get to the plane which I was told had just come in from the Isle of Sheppey. Not a lot to look at, struts and canvas and an engine plus the two pilots. The two pilots were attached to the naval flying school, and both of them were killed a week later when their machine crash landed during another demonstration. When I saw the flimsiness of the plane, there is no way that I would have gone up high above the ground in something like that.

What we did see plenty of on fine days were large, colourful balloons. They were evidently launched at Crystal Palace and usually flew or were blown over Kent on their way, hopefully, to France. On an unfavourable day, when the wind varied in direction, they could land anywhere.

But it was the lull before the storm, and our way of life was soon to be radically changed. On July 11th, Ethel and I went on the Basted Mill excursion to Ramsgate and Margate. She worked at the mill as a paper layer. It was a beautiful day, and everybody had a great time. Little did we know that in three short weeks Britain and Germany would be at war. Unfortunately for all of us and the country at large, that is exactly what happened.

France had treaties, not only with Britain but also with Russia and Serbia. Germany, as mentioned previously, was allied to the Austro-Hungarian Empire under Emperor Franz Joseph. As a result of all these treaties, if one country went to war then all would automatically be involved. In addition, Britain, France and Germany had also signed an agreement not to invade Belgium if their countries went to war against each other. It was the agreement on this piece of paper which Germany violated by going through Belgium to invade France. The attack on Belgium brought France and Britain immediately into the war against Germany. The Belgians fought gallantly from their fortified positions which they had established to protect their frontier with Germany. The Belgium troops in the forts at Namur fought very bravely; almost to the last man.

The German strategy was to attack France, conquer them very quickly and then focus their attacks on Britain. Sir Edward Grey, the Foreign Secretary, did all in his power to stop the war, but Germany just tore up the piece of paper. On August 14th, 1914, Britain and France declared war on Germany and their allies, the Austrian-Hungarian Empire. That was the end of Ethel's and my dream of getting married the following Spring. We had discussed getting married and then going on a long sea voyage to visit her father's relations in Perth, Western Australia.

August 4th, 1914, was not a very happy day for anyone; it was a Bank Holiday, rained quite a lot and I had a sense that never again would things be the same. I remember putting up a pole in the garden and running a Union Jack up it to show everybody around that we were true proud Britishers. I was twenty-three years of age, and my one brother was nineteen and a half; for the rest of my story, it will be Fred and I as our lives were closely intertwined over the next four years. We had a sister who was two years older than me and was married in 1913.

It is an understatement to say that people were stunned at the prospect of war and I know that on that Bank Holiday Monday, something inside of me died. In our spare time, after working at our jobs, Fred and I used to give our Father a hand at gathering the fruit; apples, plums, etc. as he had a small holding just outside the town, owned by Sir William Geary. Father had some lovely black diamond plums growing on tall trees, and for some reason this year these took simply ages to ripen.

A call came out from the Government in August for volunteers to enlist in the Army. Fred, with the eagerness of youth, was keen to sign-up. Lord Kitchener, who had been made Minister of War, had started a recruiting drive for one hundred thousand volunteers to train for a new Army that he needed to establish. His new army would support the British Expeditionary Force (BEF) which at that time contained the only troops Britain possessed, to send against the Germans. Once the BEF left for France, there were no reserves left in England. Some regular reserves had already been sent to India to replace professional troops serving over there. This meant the professional soldiers could be returned from India to France. Lord Roberts, 'Bobs' of India and South Africa fame, had pleaded and begged in the House of Lords from earlier in the year of 1914 that the Government should introduce conscription for the young men in my age group. The Liberal Government, however, being a peace-loving party, would not act on his warnings. There was still the view around that the BEF, which consisted of well-trained professional soldiers, would soon defeat the Germans and the troops making up the BEF would be home by Christmas. How wrong they were and how 'Bobs' was right.

Well the gallant BEF was landed in France and Belgium without any loss of life. General French, who earlier had been General Officer Commanding in Ireland, was appointed General in Charge of the BEF. But where were the Reserve Battalions or reserve troops who would be needed to replace any losses the BEF suffered? We, the future soldiers who would be required to make up the losses, hadn't even enlisted at this stage.

The British Army, to its credit, just marched and marched as far into Belgium as they could get. Finally, they encountered the German army, for it was down the Elbe valley that the Germans were attacking. The Belgians held out in their forts as long as possible which allowed the BEF a safe passage.

I met some of the soldiers who fought as part of the BEF, later in the war. They told me that the main emphasis of their training in the professional army had been to march long distances and to fire fifteen rounds rapid fire and to maintain that rate of fire for some time. The gun they used was the short magazine Lee Enfield, and I can tell you, from personal experience, that it was a fantastic rifle to use. It was said that the Germans were convinced that the British troops were using machine guns because of their rapid rate of fire. The magazines used to grow too hot to handle when used for an extended period of time in this way.

Well, the British troops got as far as Mons, but the masses of German troops opposing them forced General French to order a slow retreat. It fell to the 1st Battalion Royal West Kent Regiment to be the last regiment in the retreating army. They were ordered to fight and die if required. They had to stop the German advance in whatever way they could so as the other regiments involved in the retreat could escape.

Back in Kent, the days wore on. The plums still wouldn't ripen although the weather was sunny and warm. Fred became impatient and felt that he was missing something. On the evening of August 26th he said to me:

'I am going to enlist tomorrow whether you come with me or not; however, I would like it if you came with me.'

Hs statement put me on the spot as he obviously wanted me to enlist with him. I had more to leave behind than he had as I had plans to marry Ethel.

In the evening I went and found Ethel at her home, and we went for a walk together. I told her that Fred and I were going to enlist the following day. It was the Wednesday evening of the 26th. She took it very well, better than I thought that she would, but it was probably because she already knew that we had no alternative but to enlist.

We kissed each other, and we both felt very sad, but Lord Kitchener was still begging, on a daily basis, for one hundred thousand young men to sign-up. As it turned out it was nearly four years before we were eventually able to get married and was after I had been invalided out of the Army. Mind you I didn't even think about the possibility of getting married before Fred, and I had to leave to go to the front.

So we come to Thursday, August 27th. As I travelled to enlist I well remember seeing people gathering together to start the hop picking which was about to commence across the County; however, Fred and I had a different and more dangerous job to go to.

Chapter 2

The following day we bought return rail tickets to take us from our local station, Wrotham, to Maidstone to sign up. We were hopeful that, if we were accepted as soldiers, we would be allowed to return home that night to pick up our personal belongings. It was just a short distance up the line to the barracks of the Royal West Kent Regiment. At Wrotham Station, we bumped into a reservist from the 'E' Division of the regiment. He had just been called up and was on his way to join the Regiment. He knew the ropes so was able to guide us to the right location, which took away some of our nervousness. During our journey others, also volunteering, tagged along with us.

Up until I was fifteen and a half our family lived at Halling, and I attended a school in Snodland. Some of the men who joined us on the trip to enlist I had known from those days. Fred and I had a great time catching up on what everyone had done in the intervening years. You wouldn't have thought that we were a group about to go off to war; it was more like a school reunion. One of the guys we met was called Jim Harris. Why I mention Jim, is because, in 1918, after I had been invalided out of the army, Jim died winning the Victoria Cross while saving an officer's life. I can remember well to this day what a fine chap he was. Unfortunately, I have a lot more of those sad memories.

On arrival, we were lined up, and our basic details were written down. Next, we were all given a thorough medical examination. Fred, jokingly, had told me that he was so fit that he would have no problem passing his

medical. I went in first and was passed. Then it was Fred's turn. When he was sixteen, he had suffered a severe attack of bronchitis which slightly damaged his lungs. In the examination, his chest wouldn't expand to meet the regiment's basic requirements. The doctor rejected him. The doctor then turned to me and said:
'Are you two brothers?'
'Yes,' I replied.
'Come back here,' he signalled to Fred with a crooked finger.
This time he put the tape loosely around Fred's chest.
'Sorry young man, I seem to have made a mistake the first time. You're perfect,' he said with a smile.
Behind us was a chap with very bad eyesight. He asked me if I would whisper to him what the letters on each line of the board were during his sight test. I did that for him, and he read them out in a loud voice. He was very convincing. He was accepted, and everything went well for him until in the first few weeks of training he was asked to fire a rifle at a distant target. When he looked down the sights of the rifle, he couldn't even see the target he was expected to fire at. After a few scary moments for the rest of us, with bullets flying in all directions, he was discharged.
I was amazed that during the enlisting process nobody was asked for a birth certificate. Whatever age you gave them they wrote down. Boys of fifteen were giving their age as nineteen or twenty, and old 'uns', well over forty years old, were saying they were thirty. There were men and boys who should not have been accepted for it was a man's war they were going into. A signaller, who was with me in a dugout at the front, and who was only

seventeen, disintegrated and became a blubbering child calling for his mother when we were under shellfire in a crater in the frontline.

After the medical examination, around twenty-four of us were mustered into a room. A Magistrate, Mr Haynes, of Maidstone, was in attendance. He read out all the details of what we were committing to by signing up. Some of what he said was quite frightening. For instance, if it became necessary to shoot down members of our own family, say in a rebellion or such like, we were not expected to hesitate. After reading out the conditions of service, he gave us a few minutes to think it over. Not a single one backed out; so then he started the business of attesting us into the army. When this process was finished, he congratulated us and told us that we were now soldiers of the King for three years or for however long the war lasted.

Kitchener was reported to have said that 'given enough men and materials the war would not last longer than three years.' Others, who were supposed to know, were still saying that the war would be over by Christmas. As we now know that didn't happen. At that stage, we were afraid our big adventure would end before we could get to France.

We next went to the pay officer who gave us our pay for the day of one shilling. This amount was to be our rate of pay, the single ones anyway, for a long time to come. The married men were later given an additional one shilling a week to help support their families. Later on, when we were moved to Purfleet Rifle Range, the single chaps used to help the married ones pay their fares on the railway to go home and see their families.

After the process of enlisting, Fred and I were allowed to go home to settle up our affairs. We were instructed to be back early the next day.

The following morning we all duly arrived back at Maidstone Barracks where we were mustered by Seargent Pace. He was a veteran of the South African War or Boer War, which had ended twelve years previously in 1902. All the veterans had been promised a bonus of ten pounds if they re-enlisted. They were required to train Kitchener's New Army. Where the country would have been if theses veterans hadn't re-enlisted, I hate to think. They were fine soldiers, and just what we rookies needed to turn us into soldiers capable of fighting in France.

A few of the new recruits, we later found out, were deserters from the navy or the army. These deserters had been promised free pardons if they re-enlisted. A court of enquiry was established to judge each case on its merits, and most of them made good soldiers again.

Now Sergeant Pace, who came from Bromley in Kent, lined us up according to our height. Tom Harris was bigger and taller than Fred or I, and he was placed on our right. It then cascaded down to the smallest on the left. There were several of us there who still had to be numbered as they, 'the Army', wanted to get enough of us together to make up a platoon of forty or fifty men. When we lined up, Fred stood on my right, and Tom Harris was further up. Tom's number was 358, Fred was 363, and I was 364. Sergeant Pace then asked us which of the two of us brothers was the oldest.

'I am Sergeant,' I replied.

He made us change places so as I had a lower number than my younger brother. These were then our numbers as long as we were in the army.

Next step was to be vaccinated against smallpox and typhoid, and this was compulsory. Evidently, more soldiers died in the Boer War from Typhoid than from enemy action. We had agreed to be vaccinated in our signing on process on August 27th.

We were then taken to be fitted out with a uniform and boots etc. Most of the khaki fitted reasonably well, and I looked good in it. Unfortunately, the cap looked ridiculous which spoilt the image. We had already been issued with a badge for which we had paid sixpence, an artful transaction that. Evidently the caps required a spring in the peak to keep them up and make them look better. We were told that the tailor would supply the spring for a further two pence per cap. We soon learnt that in the Army this was the way that things worked. I found out later that those who could make a bit of extra cash always took the opportunity.

The boots we were issued with were army regulation footwear. The ones issued to me, or to be more accurate, the one for the left foot, was very tight, but there was such a shortage of equipment in those early days that I had to put up with a sore big left toe, rather than get a boot that fitted. It gradually got worse the more I wore my boots. More later about the saga of my boots.

The old soldiers and this included the 'deserters', showed us how to fold the puttees around our shins. Then we were issued with our rifles and other equipment. I was fortunate to be issued with a complete outfit. It had been collected together for a reservist who was supposed to have appeared. He, in fact, had failed to answer the call to rejoin his regiment. If what was available didn't fit or there was an item missing, that was it; there were no spares of any description. Lord Roberts had warned Mr Asquith, the Prime Minister, many times about what Germany intended to do in Europe, but the Government had ignored him, and sufficient kit hadn't been produced.

So on August 28th, we were soldiers in uniform. We were drilled for a while in formation. The drills were the same that I had been doing in school at Snodland before I left that school in 1905, but many of the veterans had never done these new drills. One man, who had been in the cavalry, told me that he used to be told to mount and that the horse then did the marching. He wasn't used to using his legs and told me he didn't like it.

We all got on pretty well together. The reports of the BEF's retreat from Mons filtered through to us, and they were not good. A very serious situation was apparently developing. There we were, the young manhood of England, learning to be soldiers. We were very far from being ready to support the BEF. If the government had listened to Lord Roberts at the start of the year, then there might have been relief troops available to increase the size of the BEF even at that early stage of the war. How that small group of soldiers, making up the BEF, stuck to the task is one of the greatest feats in the annals of the British army.

We spent two nights at the barracks and oh what a surprise we got. We went looking for mattresses only to be told there weren't any. Some of us slept on the iron beds as they were, and others, who were more experienced, slept on the floor. These harsh conditions were the beginning of more pains and discomfort than we had ever experienced before. There were a lot of very disgruntled recruits, and everybody had a good moan.

On the Sunday afternoon of August 30th, we fell in under the command of Sergeant Pace. I seem to remember that there was also an officer present. We marched to the nearest station to the Barracks and entrained for Purfleet Rifle Range. We travelled to Gravesend Central Station and then marched through the town to catch a ferry across the Thames to Tilbury.

The streets at Gravesend were lined with people cheering us and patting our backs. One big stevedore 'patted' me so hard he nearly knocked me over. He told me to kill a few Germans for him. It soon became apparent that these people thought that we were a draft on our way to France; little did they know that we were red raw and no soldiers at all. Later that evening we arrived at the Rifle Range at Purfleet. This rifle range was where most regiments around London, including the Guards, went to learn how to use their rifles.

We couldn't believe it when we were allocated to army bell tents at twenty to twenty-four men per tent. The tents had been designed to hold between ten and twelve. Again, we had to sleep on the ground and wasn't it hard. Never had my body ached so much as it did lying on the ground in those tents. I couldn't get comfortable and found it difficult to sleep. Although my work in Civvy Street was to do with the land, I didn't know how hard it was to sleep on. It certainly taught us the ability to be able to sleep anywhere, and we gradually got used to it.

Of interest was the fact that our bayonets and rifles were taken away from us almost as soon as we arrived at Purfleet. We were told that the BEF needed them in France. Taking away our rifles was a further demonstration of how badly the Liberal Government had prepared for the war. How can you go to war if you don't have the correct equipment to protect yourself? Even as raw recruits we did know that you required a gun in your hands if you were going to fight, and you also needed to know how to use it.

The effects of the vaccination were giving us considerable pain, and my left arm began to swell. Despite the discomfort, we still had to go on parades and exercises. Also, as a result of the vaccination, my brother Fred's arm, or rather his hand became septic, and it was giving him a lot of pain. He went to see the medical department at the camp, but it continued to get worse. Finally, Captain Parker, who was the officer commanding B Company, of which we were a part, told Fred to go home, see a civilian doctor and recover before he came back. The problem at Purfleet was that the doctors had all been sent to France to treat the wounded in the casualty stations there. Fred went off one Friday evening and was in a pretty bad state. I was told later by a chap who assisted him in getting from Wrotham Station to the doctor's surgery that if Fred had not gone to see the doctor at that point, he might easily have lost his hand. Well, there was Fred, a soldier in the King's army, sent home to live off his parents. There was no provision made for him for rations or pay from the regiment even though the trouble resulted from a problem he had received while enlisting. He ended up by being at home for around three months while he recovered. The local doctor was able to save most of his left thumb; however, the top part had to be amputated. When Fred rejoined us, he discovered that he was unable to work the bolt of a rifle so he couldn't use a gun.

Now Fred, I and Tom Harris plus Bill Russel and Len Mayett, who I knew as boys and also Bert Harris who I went to school with at Snodland School, were all part of 8 Platoon in B Coy. Each company had four platoons when at full strength making up around fifty men in total Captain Parker, a fine officer, had re-enlisted to take charge of our training. Sergeant Pace was the sergeant in charge, and he was also a fine and fair man. There were one or two Corporals as well. Now in 8 Platoon, we had a recruit who the chaps called 'Sailor'. His real name was Livesay, and he was a deserter from the Royal Army Medical Corps. Two or three years before the war, when he was stationed at Aldershot, he had belted a Non-Commissioned Officer, one night. He had then deserted to escape prison. His home was in Farnborough near Aldershot, so he hadn't dared to go home to see his parents since deserting in case he was arrested. Before the war, he had been working on the riverboats plying up and down the Thames under an assumed name. Because of his former job he was nicknamed 'Sailor', even though the Thames was as far as he had gone on a boat. Sailor had applied for one of the free pardons on offer, and he had been accepted. Sailor's claim to fame in the Platoon was to bolt beer and spend all his money on drink.

He wanted to go and see his mother so asked me if I would help him save his money. The idea was that he would give me half of his wages, 3/6 out of the 7/- he received each week until he had enough to pay for his fare back to Farnborough in Hampshire. Well, he duly gave me some money which I kept safe for him; however, he soon asked for it back when he ran out of money for beer. He ended up never going home. In the end, he didn't save anything and didn't go home until we all went home for Christmas.

After we had trained, and before we left for France in June 1915, Sailor was appointed the doctor's orderly and what a good job he made of it. He gave up drinking beer and devoted himself to caring for others, and, when I left the regiment in 1917, Sailor's name was highly respected. He knew his job and was totally reliable. How people can change.

Chapter 3

When we first went to Purfleet, we had no Officer allocated to our Platoon. The junior officers hadn't been trained yet. Out of the blue one day, a pleasant young officer arrived who Sergeant Pace introduced as Second Lieutenant Matthews. He had almost auburn hair and looked what he was, at least to me he did, a gentleman. We learnt that his father was a retired army officer and his home was near to Sevenoaks around the back of Knole Park. Although very young looking, the rookie officer wasn't a bit daunted by his new role. He showed us that he was going to be friendly towards us and not autocratic. Our initial impressions of him were proved correct, and he was one of us and very popular until he was sadly killed leading D Coy at the battle of the Somme on July 3rd, 1916.

Time marched on; the autumn was dry and sunny. Fred was still at home recovering from his damaged hand and the other side effects of the vaccination. I went on leave every other week and saw my parents and Ethel. You couldn't fully relax when at home because deep down inside there was always the question: 'When are we leaving for France and the war and will I survive'.

We had obviously heard that the BEF were now dug in and occupying trenches not so far from where the Germans themselves were entrenched. We also heard that the BEF were very short of reinforcements to replace the men who had already been killed or wounded. The Germans were continually attacking and causing more casualties.

Just let me say once more that everyone in Britain at that time knew that it was the courage and discipline of

General French's little army, The Old *Contemptibles*, as the Germans called them, who not only saved Britain from a German invasion but who also laid the foundation for the final victory in 1918. Of course, there was also the French Army which after initial defeats and huge losses had regrouped and helped to stop the German onslaught.

We were now well into autumn, and it was November. The rains came down and changed our camp site from passable to a disaster area. Our two blankets, at first we had only one, used to get very wet with the water seeping in under the Sides of the tent. Of course, we were still sleeping on the ground and had no way of storing our blankets above ground level. With so many in each tent, it was impossible not to touch the side, and the moisture came through. We were all thoroughly miserable.

The Commanding Officer had been appointed by now, and he was a Lieutenant Colonel, an elderly officer called Venables. His Adjutant was Captain Wingfield-Stratford, an officer taken from the 1st Battalion and he was a fine officer too. At this time there were not only 'A' and 'B' Coys but also 'C' and 'D' Coys, which made us up to a full Battalion. When we complained about the conditions we had to live in, we were told that huts were being built to house everybody at our next training location at Sandling Junction near to Hythe and Folkestone.

As November progressed and the rain continued, the grumbling got louder and more emotive. Suddenly, one really wet evening, we in our tent were huddled together trying to keep warm. We heard a lot of shouting close by and went out to investigate. There were a number of men from 'A' Coy telling us to join them in a protest at the terrible conditions that we were expected to live in. Out of curiosity, and I mean I was just curious, I went over to where the noise was, just to have a look. The rest of the chaps in 'B' Coy went with me. The leaders were calling for a revolt and wanted us to join them and give them our support. The other men of my platoon and I stayed in the background. The Adjutant and the Colonel came out of their tents and told the leaders, quite fairly, that the huts were not ready to be occupied so there was nothing that they could do for the time being as there was no available alternative.

The leaders persisted in shouting abuse at the officers. In the end, Captain Wingfield-Stratford warned everyone that if we didn't disperse that he would read the riot act and have all of us arrested. Those with common sense dispersed and went back to our tents and the riot died down. Let me make one thing very clear; I had no intention of ever causing trouble as I knew, when I signed up, that there would be hardships to endure in my life as a soldier.

Let me add that in 'C' Coy were several chaps who I knew who came from Mereworth, including a guy called Freddy Goose. He had worked with me in the gardens of Oxon Hoath in 1913. Freddy was sadly killed in the trenches near Loos in August 1915. Also, Ethel's cousin, Herbert Ashdown joined 'A' Coy. He too was killed near Arras in 1917. The Coys were gradually brought up to full strength as more and more men enlisted.

We eventually left Purfleet Rifle Range and entrained at the Range Station to travel to Sandling Junction which was close to Hythe in Kent. We went to St. Pancras Station in London and were then shunted on to the South Eastern line, as it was then called, passing through Sevenoaks, Ashford and finally arriving at Sandling Junction.

When we reached the Camp we were due to stay at; we saw what the Adjutant had told us about the state of the huts we were due to stay in was correct. Yes, there were huts; but there was no roofing felt on any of the roofs of the huts, and it was raining heavily. The contractors, in fact, were still working on the site, and there were open trenches everywhere as they were installing the sewerage system. Due to the construction work, there was mud everywhere. This new site was no better than the campsite we had left in Purfleet, in fact, it was worse. You had to wear all your clothes when sleeping. There were beds of sorts, but there were no bedclothes. Some of the men managed to sleep on the tables and the benches to get above the water. They covered themselves in the groundsheets that we were all issued with. Just before Christmas the builders finally got the huts water tight and the environment we had to live in improved considerably. The poor accommodation led to a lot of the chaps getting sick.

There was so much mud around that drilling was out of the question. The officers took us for short route marches on roads around the area. Christmas wasn't too far away, so they scheduled a week's leave for all of us. 'A' Coy went first, and it was then 'B' Coy's turn. By then it was around two weeks before Christmas Day.

I forgot to mention that Fred had rejoined us when we arrived at Sandling Junction. As he was still having problems with his hand, he was given a job by the Quartermaster in the Stores. He didn't get leave for Christmas as he had missed so much time.

I went home, and Ethel had a few days off from her work so as we could do things together. I must say I still couldn't really relax as all the time I was wondering when I would be off to France and would I ever see my home and my girlfriend again. I knew that my departure for France was getting closer but still didn't know exactly when. If I had thought about it I should have married Ethel while I was home; however, it never entered my head, and she was too polite to say anything.

News was coming through that the BEF was having an even worse time with more heavy casualties. This news didn't improve my state of mind.

The Christmas holidays over, it was decided to move the Battalion to billets in Hythe. Number 8 Platoon was accommodated in a large empty house called Cranley Court which was quite close to the seafront. The new arrangement was far better for sleeping as we were able to stay dry. We used to muster along the promenade for drills, and also we went for short route marches; however, we weren't able to do any of the parts of our training that required formal learning in a classroom. Still, we enjoyed things except that no one was allowed to go on leave, so we got a bit bored and homesick. A few of the men broke the rules and went home illegally, but most of us obeyed. On Sunday mornings we used to go to Hythe Church to their Sunday Service. The people there were very warm and friendly.

The next step in the development of the Battalion was that people were asked to volunteer for specialist jobs. I was interested in becoming a Signaller, so I put my name forward. The instructor for the signallers was a local man called Sergeant Dale. His regular job was Postman, and he lived close by. He selected sixteen of us, four from each Coy, and we were trained outside on the green close to his house. It was all semaphore, so we had to learn the Morse Code, plus signalling using small flags. He was an excellent teacher, and also a nice man, we enjoyed being trained by him. Semaphore was more commonly used by the Royal Navy, but it did have a use at that time in the Army.

It was nice to be different to all the other recruits who only had to use a rifle and a bayonet, and I felt important. Fred rejoined the Platoon but was still far from fit with his thumb as it was.

Another major grumble started amongst the men. There was a severe shortage of food, and a lot of the recruits were going hungry. They complained that someone was nicking their rations. It became serious and threatened to get out of hand so Lieutenant Matthews said that he would hold an enquiry at Cranley Court. Those that were the most vociferous in their complaints got the wind up when they heard that they would have to make a formal complaint to an officer. Now Fred and I hadn't said anything as we got food parcels from home on a weekly basis and didn't go hungry. Lieutenant Matthews duly came to hold the enquiry accompanied by Sergeant Pace. The moaners got stage fright and asked me if I would go in and explain to the officer what the problem was. Well, I agreed to represent them as long as it was made clear that I wasn't one of the trouble makers, so in I went. Lieutenant Matthews was surprised to see me and asked me what my complaint was.

'I don't have any complaint, Sir,' I replied.

'Then why are you here Kemp?' he asked, looking at me slightly puzzled.

'No sir, it is that lot outside who are complaining, but they are afraid to speak to you, so they asked me to represent them.'

'Well now that you are here, can you please tell us what all this is about,' the Lieutenant said.

'The rations that we are getting aren't enough to fill us, and we are always hungry, Sir.'

'But we haven't cut down the amount of food that is issued.'

'The men believe that some of the food is being stolen or is going missing,' I added.

'Alright Kemp, leave it with me, and I will look into it. Is that all?'

'Yes Sir, that is all.'

When I left him the mob outside were all eager to hear what had transpired and what the verdict was. I told them to bloody well go and find out for themselves. In fact, we soon started to get more food, and the problem went away. Rumour had it that the wives and hangers-on of some of Non-Commissioned Officers were living off our rations and that this was common practice at Army bases in both England and overseas.

We remained at Hythe until the end of February. Our small group of signallers continued to learn Morse Code with flags, but we also had to go on longer marches with the Battalion. My big toe began to get very sore and was extremely painful each time that I went on a march. I went to the doctor a few times when marches were scheduled and got excused. One day the doctor got very angry as he had such a lot of 'lead swingers' as he called them. His answer to the problem was to put everyone on a crime sheet, including myself. In the afternoon I had to appear before Captain Towse, the second in command, to answer a charge of malingering. My platoon officer, Lieutenant Matthews, somehow was able to prove to the Officer Commanding that I was one of the best fellows in his platoon and that I was genuinely in a bad way with my toe. Well, Captain Towse had served in South Africa during the second Boer War with the celebrated City Imperial Volunteers and started lecturing me about keeping my boots soft by dubbening them. No one had the sense to see that my left boot wasn't big enough for my foot. It could have simply been that I had been issued with odd boots. I still had to march, and my toe got worse and worse being very raw after a long distance. I have a bunion on my left big toe to this day as a memorial to the ignorance of those in command. Later on, at Aldershot, before leaving for France, I was able to get a pair of boots big enough for my foot to stretch in, but, even after I got the new boots my foot never stopped hurting when marching and we did a lot of that in the Army.

At the end of our time in Hythe, we were told that we would be marching in stages to Aldershot. Also marching to Aldershot by different routes would be the 6th Buffs, the 6th Queen's Royal West Surreys and the 7th East Surrey Regiment.

The first day we marched to Ashford where we were billeted in private houses for the night. The next day we marched to Rolvenden where we were accommodated in huge barns that were empty and beautifully built. We were not allowed to smoke inside the barn. The next night we stayed at Tenterden where there were magnificent trees lining the street. From there we went to Tunbridge Wells. Now it was Thursday in Tunbridge Wells, and we were paid our wages. My home was only twelve miles away so I asked a pal named Wager if he would like a ride home with me. The roads were covered with a few inches of frozen snow. We each hired a bicycle for a shilling, and off we went. Sergeant Pace saw us and guessed what we were up to, but he didn't stop us.

We made March Farm, West Peckham, but it was hard going on the snowy roads. I left Wager to sit beside the fire with my parents and cycled the two and a half miles to Ethel's home. You've guessed right; it was my beautiful girl that was the purpose of my trip all along and not my parents. We hadn't had a pass home since the Christmas break. After a while with Ethel, I cycled home, and we slept having told my father to wake us up at 4.30am. He gave us some breakfast and mother gave us a cake to take with us. We set off in darkness, but it soon got light, and we were just back at our billet when Sid Mundey, our bugler, blew the reveille. My legs and bum ached from the cycle ride, and the pain was made worse as we had to march ten miles that day; however, seeing Ethel was worth all the aches and pains that I had to endure.

By Sunday evening we reached Godalming, and this lovely village, nestling at the bottom of the hill, has stayed in my mind since that time in 1915. By Monday morning we were ready for the final stage into Aldershot. As we joined the main road which we took to bring us past Farnborough, Sailor showed us the house where his mother lived. Being closer to his home meant that Sailor, at last, would be able to visit his mother.

Chapter 4

When we arrived at Aldershot Camp, we were allocated to Alberara Barracks which was a vast improvement on what we had to endure before when accommodated at Army Camps. We had plenty of living space, and we were able to keep dry. But now the full course of training commenced, and for the next three months, we were to undergo vigorous training activities. This meant longer and longer marches until we were able to do the full thirty-one miles which was the required distance expected of us in one day. Where this exact distance came from was a mystery to us all.

After a few weeks we Signallers, together with members of the band; yes we had a band, were housed together in a Barrack room of our own. We learnt that at the front in Flanders, they had dispensed with flags and semaphore and were now using telephones. We obviously had to change our whole method of operation, so we were issued with field telephones which we called 'buzzers'. When on manoeuvres we had to run out the wires to the various companies, and we were congratulated on doing a good job with the new system. On many of the trials running out wires that we did at Aldershot, our journey took us into Berkshire. Towards the end of our stay, we were engaged in mock warfare with bayonets and rifles and the troops charging through trees, etc. We often came across men from other regiments doing the same. It appeared to be chaos at times as often we almost met other charging troops; however, just before we collided and started mowing each other down the Umpire would blow his whistle and stop us just in time

Time passed, and we became fitter and more experienced. We were given four days leave around the middle of May, and, although I didn't say anything to Ethel or my parents, I sensed that they knew it was the last leave before we would depart for France and the trenches.

We were all back at Aldershot by the third week of May when one final 'show' was arranged. We were to stay out in the open for forty-eight hours and look after ourselves for that time. There were plenty of wide open spaces in Hampshire and Berkshire where this exercise was going to happen. To crown it all we were told that King George V and Queen Mary, would be waiting about one mile out of Aldershot to take the salute. We halted a short distance before the spot where the review was to take place, and Sergeant Dale, 'Tommy' to everyone, our signal Sergeant, looked at me said that I looked decidedly unwell. He was right; I did feel very unwell. Sergeant Dale told the Regimental Sergeant Major, and he ordered me to go to the Camp for treatment.

He said: 'We trust you to go back on your own Kemp, so off you go.'

So instead of seeing their Majesties, I trudged back to the Barracks on my own. A doctor looked at me and sent me immediately to Cambridge Military Hospital which was a lovely place. I was put to bed, and the doctor said that I had a bad dose of flu. Flu in those days was often fatal.

The Regiment returned to Barracks and Fred came to see me. During my time in the hospital, the rest of the fellows in the Regiment had their medical examination to pass them fit for overseas service.

I was back with them just over a week later but hadn't had my medical examination. I asked Lieutenant Matthews; he had been promoted to be a full Lieutenant recently:

'When will I have my medical examination, Sir?'

'Do you want to go with us?' he replied.

'Of course, I do,' I said.

'Well let's just say that you passed.'

I was surprised with his answer but accepted that I was going with the rest of them. I have wondered since how many men went overseas, as I did, without a medical examination. So these were the last few days in England for us.

We were told that no-one would be allowed out of camp and that no letters would be forwarded until after we left England. It was explained that there must be no chance of information reaching the German Submarines that we were going across the Channel on a specific date.

We were then a part of 12 Division, the Ace of Spades Division. This unit was made up of twelve regiments, besides artillery and all other sections. On Saturday, which incidentally was a beautiful day, Lieutenant Matthews paid for his entire platoon, the 8th, to have their photo taken in a group with him sitting in the middle. He then got all the addresses of where we wanted to have our copy of the photo sent. Many of those chaps never saw their photos as they died before they got their first leave from France, but at least their family had a picture of their son or husband in uniform.

Our lengthy preparation was now over, and we were about to take part in the real affair which was fighting against the Germans. Our Division was one of the first of the new Divisions to actually be sent to France and most of us, with the exception of seven officers and some Non-Commissioned Officers, were civilians before August 1914. We were very well aware that the BEF needed help, so we went away, not unhappy, but curious as to the outcome of it all. To me, at that time, death didn't seem possible as most of us felt that we would be spared to return home again. Alas, the toll of the brave men of Kent from our regiment was very large as can be seen when you read all the names on the Memorials situated in the Cemeteries in France and Belgium.

On Monday I was ordered to proceed overseas with the transport which was to leave before the main Battalion as I had been riding one of the bicycles allocated to Signallers. So early Monday morning, without any fuss, we went down to the little railway station of Fleet, entrained quickly under the command of Major Beeching, the Battalion's second in command, and headed for Southampton.

It was May 31st, 1915, and we completed our journey to Southampton without alarms. We then all helped in loading the horses and mules, general service waggons, water carts and all the baggage aboard the transport ship Maileran which was an old iron vessel. It looked as if it had been used to transport cattle in the pre-war years. We left Southampton at 6.00pm. I gather the Captain had been told by the destroyer escort that there were mines in the Channel, so the Captain didn't take a direct course. The skipper heard that there were Signallers amongst the party and he asked for two men to go up onto the bridge to pick up the semaphore signals which the escorting destroyers were giving us. I was one of the men allocated to go to the bridge. So there were two rookies up on the bridge with the Captain. He managed to read the signals a lot quicker than we did but he seemed to like having our company and we, in turn, liked being up on the bridge as it was a lovely night. We went around the Isle of Wight and headed for Le Havre where we arrived at about 3.00am on June 1st. We disembarked later that day and then marched to the rest camp which was situated on a hill above the port six miles away. We spent the night there.

Three days later we entrained to travel to Boulogne where we were to meet the bulk of the Regiment who duly joined our train. We then departed for a place called Esquerdes. We then waited a further three days for the remainder of the Battalion to come from Aldershot to Boulogne. On the Monday that we, the advanced party, left Aldershot, there was a parade at which the Commanding Officer and other notables inspected the Battalion and offered their congratulations for the success of the training. Two chaps were called out to go and speak to the Colonel, one was a little ginger headed chap called Mitchley, and the other was my brother Fred. Mitchley was offered his ticket out of the army because he was so weak and small. Fred, my brother, was offered the option to leave because he only had half a thumb on his left hand and couldn't work the bolt of a Lee Enfield. Mitchley said that he wanted to go with the Regiment as his brother had been killed during the retreat from Mons and there was a debt that he wanted to pay. Fred said that he wanted to go because that was what he had joined up and trained for. Both of them were allowed to go back to their places and could go to France. Almost immediately Lieutenant Matthews, our Platoon Officer, made Fred his orderly and servant, thereby making it easier for Fred to live and be of use. He remained in that job when Lieutenant Matthews was made up to Captain and Officer Commanding 'D' Coy. Unfortunately, as mentioned before, the Captain was killed on the Somme during the attack on July 3rd, 1916. At the same time, Fred was wounded and was sent back to a hospital in Nottingham.

Now I must go back to our stay at Aldershot. A few weeks before we departed for France, we were all fitted out with new uniforms. They were the first replacements that we had received since being issued with the first kit at Maidstone in August 1914 and our uniforms were a bit the worse for wear. We were also given new grey shirts. These shirts were woollen, so we no longer had to wear a vest. Neither did we wear underpants as we were told that our life was going to be tough. We would have to wear our clothes for long periods, and the body lice would cause us a lot of grief. We only found out about the body lice at a later date. Much to my delight, we were also issued with new boots. Mine, this time, fitted me a treat, but the damage had already been done and my left big toe was still sore when I marched, which was a lot of the time. We were also issued with a new rifle and equipment. Inside the uppers of each of our boots, our rank, name, Regimental number and Regiment name was stamped. The same was done with our rifle.

To return to my story. A couple or three years after the end of the war, say 1920 or 1921, my brother Fred, who like me was a civilian again after being demobbed, received a letter from the War Office asking if he could remember swapping his boots with another soldier while we were serving in the Armentières sector in 1915. The letter said that a British soldier's body had been dug up from where he died to be relocated to one of the cemeteries. His boots had Fred's name, rank and number on them. The letter said that they had found out from our Regiment that Fred was alive, but, could he remember the name of the soldier who he exchanged his boots with! Fred wrote back saying that he was sorry but he didn't know that his boots were ever exchanged. This extraordinary situation meant that another soldier's name was omitted from the nearest War Memorial in Flanders close to where they found the body.

Now, previous to our departure from Aldershot, we were asked to write down what we had done in civilian life prior to enlisting. Why they asked this I never knew for as far as I was concerned I was a soldier of the King until further notice. Corporal Piper, a Londoner by birth, but also an old soldier from the South African campaign, came around to take down the details from everyone. He came to a quiet little chap who had recently joined us.

'What was your occupation in civilian life?' Corporal Piper asked him.

'Burglar,' said the little man.

'I asked you what your occupation was in civilian life?' the Corporal asked again.

'I told you. I was a burglar,' the little man repeated.

He went on to explain that he had always been a burglar. He had never worked and had never been caught; yet.

This man went with us to Flanders, but I have no idea how he fared there. I also have no idea what the Corporal wrote down in his book.

When we arrived at our destination in France, I was attached to Headquarters Battalion and was no longer with the Platoon.

Now we had another man join us; I would say that he was getting on for forty years of age. He was a quiet type and came from Chatham. Now this gentleman and gentleman he always was, had been the Chief Artificer at the Chatham Dockyard where all the submarines were built. He told us that he had been in charge of his part of the work on all the trials of submarines. I never understood how men of his level of skill and importance were allowed to leave their job and become an ordinary foot soldier. I have forgotten this man's name, but he stayed with us until early in 1916 when he was detailed to leave the Regiment, who were at that time serving in the trenches. He wasn't allowed to tell us where he was being sent. I have always had a suspicion that this man was taken to a spot behind the lines and was somehow involved in the arrival of the first tanks that were used in September and October at Flers on the Somme battlefield.

The part of England from which the Queens Own West Kents were drawn from started, say, south of the Thames at Greenwich, through Deptford and the docks area, across to Dulwich, through Beckenham, Bromley, Sevenoaks, Tonbridge, Tunbridge Wells, across to Maidstone, over the North Downs incorporating

Rochester, Chatham and Gillingham. The rest of Kent, which included Thanet and to the South of Maidstone was the territory of the Buffs, the East Kent Regiment and we, the civilian recruits, just joined the home regiments of our area.

There was an even split in the numbers who enlisted from London and the country districts. The Londoners were very sharp-witted and quick movers. Many of us from the country may have been slower in talking, but what a blend we made, and that is why all through the war the Queens Own Battalions stood high in the respect of others. In our spare time many games of cards were played, some for money if chaps had money, on other occasions cigarettes and matches were the stakes. I very seldom played for money for to see how those boys from London could shuffle a pack of cards and bring out a queen whenever they liked, just proved to me that I couldn't win against them. When we were in the trenches at the quiet time, we, on 'B' Coy phone, Sid Durden, Jack Webb, two from London, and myself, enjoyed a game of cards.

In 'B' Coy we had a Londoner called Gus Ball. Gus ran a crown and anchor board and being very smart, but always playing very fair in his dealings, won considerably. We had a Sergeant by the name of Kerslake, Jimmy to us, and he was also from London. He became the Quartermaster Sergeant of B Coy and was responsible for our rations being delivered even when we were in the trenches. He used to come up to the trenches and make sure that the food was delivered fairly. Now, believe it not, Jimmy's father was a German who had come over to London to open a bakery business. We all liked him and found him to be an honest and fair chap. Whether we liked the Germans who we were fighting against is another story. Jimmy Kerslake was one of the kindest and most loyal of friends one could have, especially while in the trenches. It just proves that wars are not between the natives of the different countries but wars are between politicians and Kings.

Reflections Chapters 1 to 4

The declaration of War on August 14th, 1914 found Great Britain not so 'great' and totally unprepared for a serious war. In the last eight years before war was declared, the Liberal Government had been involved in very 'noble' projects directed at improving the lot of the lower paid workers and pensioners. These were vote-winning projects to keep them in power. They should have been spending an equivalent amount of time enhancing the military capability of the country as the experts said that there was a high likelihood of war with Germany. Very simply, they had been involved in improving the conditions for the electorate rather than in preparing for war. In the mind of the politician, there was always the possibility and hope that war wouldn't actually arrive. If they were proved wrong, then there would be a lot of catching up to do.

The only area where sufficient attention and funds seem to have been applied, was in the upgrading of the Fleet to counteract what the Kaiser was doing to the German Navy. A large number of Dreadnought battleships had been ordered from British Shipbuilders by the Department of Defence and had rolled off the slipways in a very short space of time.

Sid Kemp's description of England in the years just before war was declared, paints a very realistic picture of the life facing most inhabitants of the British Isles in those days. He was clearly from the working class whose total focus was on survival and eking out a living.

The Officer Class was a world apart from the lower echelons of society and the only time that the two classes met was as Lord and Servant. While the working man was concerned about daily survival; they lived in very basic accommodation, the Officer Class were more concerned about keeping up appearances. In many cases, an Officer would have to spend money to maintain his position in the Regiment. It was often the case that you only gained promotion in a Regiment if you could afford to exist at the next level. And, for goodness sake don't pass the port the wrong way around the dinner table! Slowly, changes were being made in the social structure of the Army and the old rules governing the Officer Class were at last changing. The First World War brought the old way of operating to a shuddering halt as a bullet killed an officer just as it did a Private; it wasn't selective. In fact, in the early stages of the war, the German Snipers used to target the officers by aiming for those wearing the Sam Browne belt. Officers when they realised that they could be easily identified by the belt, stopped wearing their Sam Browne belt into battle.

Unfortunately, the older senior officers were stuck in the past and could only draw on their own experiences. The age profile of this group was between fifty-five and sixty-five years of age. Set in their ways, it was nearly impossible for them to change to meet the demands of a modern military conflict. It was all new to them, and all they could do was throw men at the problem while they thought of another way of meeting the challenges of a battle.

The Crème de la Crème in the British Army was the Cavalry Regiment. It cost more to be an officer in these Regiments than it did in the Infantry, so you required private means to exist. It is fair to say that the Cavalry

Officers looked down on the Officers from the ordinary Regiments. The senior officers had also learnt their trade and tactics in the Commonwealth, with the most recent battles having taken place in South Africa, around the turn of the century.

In 1914 the total compliment of the Army was around one hundred and sixty thousand men. In recent times no Generals had managed a force of more than a fraction of this number. The systems and controls in place were only meant to handle an Army of this size. Methods of Communication were also somewhat primitive and would prove to be the Achilles Heel of the BEF. In the past, the Cavalry did a lot of the gathering of intelligence. The men at the top had all come through the system and all thought in a particular way. It was as if they had all been made in the same mould; they all looked the same and titles were the only thing that made them different and how they loved their titles. For instance, General French was very upset and felt ridiculed when he was Commander in Charge of the BEF and Field Marshal Kitchener visited him. Kitchener was wearing the uniform of a Field Marshal which outranked French at the time as he was only a General.

To have expected the Generals to be original thinkers is unrealistic as they didn't rise through the system by being out of the box thinkers. In fact, any officer on the way up the ladder who showed character and originality was likely to be kept down and put in his place. The older Generals were afraid of being shown up, so made sure that original thinkers, and those who showed initiative, weren't part of their staff. The situation between General French and General Smith-Dorrien, early on in the conflict, is a case in point.

In the first four chapters of Sid's story, there are some interesting facts that I am sure the discerning reader will have picked up.

You would think that Field Marshall Lord Roberts would have been listened to when he said that it was time to start the recruitment process at the beginning of the year of 1914. There was already talk of war at that stage, but the politicians ignored all the signs as it didn't fall in line with their own agendas. Lord Roberts was very vociferous in the House of Lords about the small number of troops that were available should the country go to war. His main point being that it would take at least nine months to turn a civilian into a front line soldier. In fact, nothing was done until war was declared, so there were no new recruits signed up, until August 1914. Add on the nine month's training, and that meant that new troops wouldn't be available to join the BEF until May of 1915. Fortunately, the main Commonwealth countries were able to send some trained troops to support the BEF. This input just about kept the numbers at a satisfactory level until Kitchener's New Army was ready to travel to the battlefield.

When the young men enlisted, they were not in a satisfactory physical condition to tackle the Germans. The food required for building muscle and physique was in short supply in most working-class families in England. Those enlisting were considerably underweight and physically weak. It would take the men who enlisted in August 1914 a few years to achieve a satisfactory physical state to be able to take on the Germans in hand to hand warfare on an equal footing. The Germans were all conscripts and had spent two years compulsory service in the army prior to war breaking out in August 1914. They had been fed lots of the right sort of food during their two years of training and were consequently physically more robust and fitter.

Of perhaps greater significance was the fact that the materials required to fight a war weren't available. Rifles, artillery and shells were all in short supply. In addition, the uniforms and boots that the new recruits would have to wear were also lacking. Sid Kemp was issued with two boots of different sizes, one of which was far too small. He was then expected to go on long route marches which damaged his left foot. He had a problem with his left foot for the rest of his life.

Having been given rifles in Maidstone, when they enlisted, these were taken away from them a little while later as there was evidently a shortage in France. Not a very morale boosting action for the new recruits who wanted to be soldiers. Soldiers expected to fight without guns!

I don't know whether the poor conditions that the recruits had to live in were a deliberate strategy to make them get used to the conditions they were likely to face in the trenches. The fact that there were no mattresses and in some cases no beds, so they had to sleep on the floor, made them get used to sleeping on anything. Personally, I don't think that the powers that be were capable of thinking with that sort of creativity, but I will give them the benefit of the doubt that the shortcomings in the living conditions were a planned strategy.

One of the most alarming situations that was allowed to develop was caused by the after effects of the vaccination for Smallpox and Typhus. Sid had a slight reaction, but his brother Fred had an appalling reaction which necessitated him going home for three month's to recover. He was sent home to his parents, and no provision was made to pay him. The cost of his recovery, including medical charges, had to be borne by his parents. When he eventually returned to his regiment, he was in a state where he couldn't fight as he was unable to manipulate the bolt of a rifle.

Sid was very upset that boys as young as sixteen were allowed to sign up. They were desperate for new recruits to increase the size of Kitchener's Army but taking young men of that young age was a betrayal to their mothers. It was a big adventure for the boys as none of them had been out of England. In fact, in most cases, they had never been out of the district where they were born and reared. You only have to look at the tombstones in the War Cemeteries of Northern Europe to see how many of these boys never returned home. There were also men over forty who enlisted but they knew what they were getting into and one can't feel the same sympathy for them.

The last point I would like to make here is that the planning that was done before they took on the recruits seemed to have been minimal. The camps, where the men were accommodated while they undertook their training, were wholly inadequate. The location was so poor that they were unable to carry out a lot of the training, making the whole exercise futile. Putting twenty-four recruits in a tent which had been designed to hold twelve; and in the middle of winter, was not very smart.

I have highlighted a few points here, but you can come to your own conclusions having read Sid Kemp's account of what he had to go through.

Let's return to his story.

Chapter 5

I would like to jump forward now to the launch of the offensive called The Battle of the Somme which took place in July 1916. In the time that we had been in France, Gus Ball had accumulated £100 in profit from his 'Crown and Anchor' board. Knowing that his chances of survival were small when he had to go over the top, Gus gave his money to Jimmy and asked him to send it home to his wife in London if anything happened to him. Well, Gus left us, as so many did on that terrible morning of the July 3rd, 1916. No more was thought about Gus's money, at least by me, until June 1917. I had been lucky not to be on the end of a bullet until suddenly my health deteriorated, and in April 1917, I found myself a patient in a Military Hospital in Brighton. More about what actually happened later. Originally, it had been the Workhouse, but it had now been converted into a Hospital. The property overlooked the racecourse, but there were no race meetings during the war years.

I spent several weeks at the Hospital before I was well enough to be allowed to take a ride on a tram which in Brighton gave free rides to all the boys dressed in hospital blue. The very first time that I went out, which was on a Sunday, I got off at the Aquarium and walked across the road to the Promenade. Who did I bump into but Gus Ball. He was leaning against the railings supported by a pair of crutches. He only had one leg. How pleased we were to see each other and after a while, I asked him whether Jimmy Kerslake sent his money back to his wife after we thought that he had been killed. He said that the money had arrived a few days after he had been wounded. Gus was a patient at the Royal Pavilion Hospital which did so much for those who lost limbs during the war. I never met Gus again during my stay in Brighton. Seeing all those maimed and young men suffering in Brighton made me wonder whether all the killing and maiming was really necessary in the great scheme of things. Surely the politicians could have sorted out their differences without going to war against each other. It was all so senseless. None of the politicians was there recovering from shell damage to their bodies!

I feel that I need to pay a special tribute to Sergeant Dale, 'Tommy', our signal Sergeant. At the outbreak of the war, Sergeant Dale reported to the depot in Maidstone in the early days as he was an 'A' class Reservist. He was taken out of a draft that was leaving immediately to reinforce the 1st Battalion now over in France. Being a signalling non-commissioned officer, he was held back to teach Morse Code and semaphore to chaps, who, like me, were now in the 6th Battalion. He attempted to make signallers out of us. Now the Sergeant was an excellent teacher; he was also a Londoner which made him streetwise. He managed to get the signallers billeted together at Aldershot. He told us that in his experience in the Army, even in peacetime, the other fellows resented those who got on and took it out on them, so we were better kept separate. I could agree with him as personally, I found that I didn't get on with my regular mates when we had to billet with 8 Platoon in Hythe. They were jealous.

After a while in France, Sergeant Dale somehow got us transferred to Headquarters Company that included the Runners. These chaps took messages that were too private to send over the phones. Also, in cases of emergency, they had to take messages for relief back to HQ when a platoon was in trouble, and the telephone lines were broken. The Signallers in our Battalion always marched ahead of the rest of the Battalion with Regimental Sergeant Major Lawson, another very fine soldier. He was retired when the war broke out, but came back and kept superb discipline in all ranks. Being with the Signallers, made life a lot easier for me in those early days in France and the trenches. All the rest of the Company had to go back and work in the trenches area when they were relieved from holding the line, but the signallers were allowed to improve their knowledge of signalling. So life for us was that much easier. It appeared that those in authority wanted us to be fresh for the job that we had to do. Sunshine or rain the fellows had to return to the trenches doing such jobs as rebuilding parapets, carrying duckboards, which were used to walk on in the wet trenches, and doing carrying for the miners who were burrowing under the German lines where ever it was possible to create a mine. The earth had to be taken away from the frontline and spread around behind so as the Germans wouldn't spot the tunnelling. I must make it clear that they did this support work after they had been relieved from the front line by another Regiment. Working parties, usually from the same Company, were sent back to work helping the Regiment in the line. These parties did say four or five hours each day but not at night time. The working parties usually had an officer in charge and a platoon sergeant. All had to wear battle dress which consisted of all equipment less the backpack, which almost always carried our greatcoat, washing and other personal things. During the summer of 1915 this was regular practice; however, later on, when it came to winter, and the trenches were in a bad way, it was impossible to go back and work,

I've got ahead of myself, so I must go back in time again. We disembarked at Le Havre on the afternoon of June 1st. We had no trouble in getting the horses, mules and equipment ashore, so it didn't take too long to unload. We then marched through the town with a lot of young boys running beside us looking for bully beef. As we only had been issued with one day's rations, we were unable to give them any. It was an amazing comfort to hear the kids talking to us in English; we felt that we were among friends.

We marched about four miles to a rest camp outside the port of Le Havre and then spent one more day resting. We entrained the following day to travel to Boulogne where we were to meet the rest of the Battalion on June 3rd. We then travelled by train to a place called Esquedes, where we stayed the night. Next morning we left Esquedes and marched on roads as we had done in England; however, this time the roads were constructed from cobblestones. The cobbles were very hard on our feet, and we all got blisters. Well, we marched around twelve miles that day and wasn't I relieved when we arrived at a place called Sercus after that dreadful march. I remember Captain Dawson, the second in command of 'C' Coy, and of immortal fame later on in the battalion's history, carrying nine or ten fellows' rifles to enable them to keep marching. He was that sort of officer and had indomitable courage.

Our objective was a place called Meteren, a relatively large village with a parish church a few hundred yards to the south. Just before we entered the village, I saw the only hop garden that I ever saw in France. There was a large brewery close by at Armentières. Between the road, that we were marching on and the hop garden were the graves of several soldiers. These were the first graves of soldiers that we had come across. When we asked the villagers what had happened, this is the story that they told us.

After the BEF fell back from Mons and the Germans kept following them, the order came from General French to stand and fight. It appeared that the BEF retreated to the south of Meteren, then they turned, and it was now the Germans that were retreating. The Germans had placed a machine gun at the top of the square church tower. From there they had an uninterrupted view of the approaches to the street running through the centre of the village. When the British troops came marching up the road, the German machine gun just mowed the front ranks down. This tragedy was the reason why the graves were so close to the road and adjoining the hop garden. The French people told us that the rest of the British soldiers surrounded the church and rushed up the stairs. They threw, not only the machine gun but also the gun crew from the top of the church tower to their deaths. The people of Meteren hated the German for what they had done, but of course, it was war.

By June, the weather was sunny and we signallers were billeted at a small farm. It seemed to us that all farms in France were small with only a few acres. We put our groundsheets up to make a sort of tent, and we then slept out in an orchard. When we had been at Meteren for a couple of days or so, I was detailed to go to Baillieu, find the Town Major, and arrange with him for baths for the Battalion. I was still using one of the bicycles as out of the sixteen signallers there were very few who were able to ride a bike. Most of the ones who couldn't ride were from London where they had no need of one. In the country we needed one to get around, and I used to cycle to work.

I also used to take the Commanding Officer's night report to Brigade Headquarters which was about three or four miles away. One night, and it was past midnight, I was passing the East Surry Headquarters but didn't have any lights showing. Suddenly, out of the darkness, came a challenge to halt and a bayonet flashed past me. I accelerated and certainly didn't dare stop. On my way back I went slowly looking for the sentry. I found him and with him was the Sergeant of the guard. I stopped and asked them to curb their enthusiasm as the challenge came after the bayonet was lunged at me. We laughed over it and said a cheery goodnight to one another. Afterwards, when I had to take the report to Headquarters, I was always careful of 'windy' sentries.

I want now to give you some facts about food and cooking.

Each Coy was provided with a portable kitchen capable of cooking food for two hundred men, but the Battalion Headquarters was provided with a cook, by name, not by ability to cook. He cooked for us signallers and the other staff at BHQ. Now an old soldier called Nobby Clarke; all Clarkes were called Nobby in the army, was detailed to do our cooking. Where Nobby learned to cook, I never found out, but, his cooking was pretty crude to be kind. There was also a saying that all army cooks used to chew tobacco as well as smoke it. Many men in those days, working on the land and at hard jobs used to have the same bad habit. The dinner that Bobby cooked us was always a stew. He used to cut the meat into pieces, put it in a cold Dixie, add water and then try and cook it. Some days it was edible, and some days it wasn't. Now I know for a fact that Nobby used to chew tobacco and yet I never saw him do what a lot of other cooks did; if the tobacco they were chewing was tough, they used to spit it into the Dixie. The gravy that Nobby made sometimes had a bad taste. I wonder was it tobacco flavoured.

Luckily we were always ravenous and were glad to get anything. After Lieutenant Matthews had made my brother Fred a servant and orderly, he was able to get me the odd tin of bully beef and Machonices. These made a welcome change to my normal diet, especially when we were in the trenches.

Now while we were at Meteren, where we stayed about two weeks, I had two offers which could have changed my life. First, one day as I was riding my bicycle down the main street of Meteren, I met Lieutenant Matthews, my old officer of 8 Platoon and the officer Fred looked after. He asked me to leave the signallers and come back to the Platoon. He said that he would make me up to Corporal with immediate effect. I told him that I was happy to stay with the signallers based at BHQ, but he asked me to think about his offer. A few days later, Sergeant Dale, our signal sergeant, told me that he had recommended me to be permanently posted to Divisional Headquarters to represent the Battalion there. They had decided that one member of each regiment in the Division was required to be based at Division HQ to do light duties there and for ceremonial occasions. The person appointed would not have to do duty in the trenches anymore. In fact, it would be a wonderful life; plenty to eat, and always somewhere comfortable to sleep. He wanted me to accept, but I told him that I couldn't let my brother go to the trenches while I took an easy way of life. I refused and felt that I was doing the right thing. About a year later I met the chap who went to Divisional HQ in my place. He looked to be in perfect health and was pleased he had got the job. Still, I kept faith with myself and my choice of job.

Besides having cookers, the Battalion also had two large water carts, each pulled by a horse. In charge of the water carts was another old soldier by the name of Wood. He was known to all as 'Bungey'. He was an artist, and I would think could have earned good money working as one in civilian life. Everywhere we stayed in Flanders, Bungey would look for a nice piece of blank wall on a house or building, or even on the door of a shed and he would draw a large picture of our cap badge, the rampant horse. This practice was followed by many regiments; once started it went on and on. Later, when we were to be issued with steel helmets in 1916, Bungey drew the design of a cap badge, the same size as we wore on our caps, and this design was stamped on the camouflage material which was stretched over the helmet. The material was to stop the glitter so as German snipers wouldn't see them. I have still got the memory after all these years at seeing Bungey drawing a beautiful picture of Kent's famous horse on a wall.

We had a signaller from 'C' Coy called Mitchell, a nice enough chap but a bit impetuous. Which, in my opinion, is what cost him his life a few weeks later. Now Mitchell was out by himself one day in Meteren when he met an elderly Frenchman riding in a little cart drawn by a dog. Seeing the dog being maltreated upset Mitchell as he was a dog lover. He ordered the poor little Frenchman, who, by the way, didn't speak a word of English, to get out of the cart and pull it himself. The meeting of the two developed into a major row until somebody came along who spoke both French and English and he was able to explain to Mitchell that this was common practice in this part of France. It was then settled by handshakes. Mitchell explained that he had been very upset at seeing the dog pulling the man in the cart along the road. Dogs were also used to draw water from shallow wells with the Chateau type of house using the dogs to tread the wheel. I used to feel very sorry for these dogs as they were hemmed in and couldn't get away. They had to keep treading until enough water had been drawn from the wells. The water system was non-existent as we knew it in England and we had been warned, when we landed, only to drink the water provided from our water carts. This water was chlorinated, usually with too much of the chemicals, so it wasn't very pleasant.

Chapter 6

It was now the month of June, and back home in Kent, our parents had fresh strawberries. Now for some strange reason, I didn't like strawberries, and my parents were well aware of this fact. Unusual I know, but I had never liked them. For some reason, only known to themselves, they decided to send me some fresh strawberries as a special treat. They picked about six pounds of fruit, packed them in a cardboard box and posted the package to me. I never did find out why they didn't send them to Fred as he loved them. But read on to see what happened.

At the front, we had a middle-aged postman who looked after our mail. He had been given the job as he was a postman in civilian life. I can't remember his name or where he came from. One day, while we were still at Meteren, he went with the general service waggon to the railhead at Steinwert to collect the Battalion's mail. Well, as is the regular practice, the mail for each company was placed in separate bags and, of course, the mail for Headquarters was in its own bag. Usually, the postman only had to pick up his specific bag of mail and get going. This particular day there was a big mess caused by a package of strawberries in a cardboard box. Beside the, by now, very messy pink coloured box were all the letters for the Commanding Officer, the Adjutant, etc. It appears that the juice had seeped through the mailbag. Our postman had to sort through all the letters and try to wipe the pink juice off the envelopes before he brought them to Headquarters. When he arrived at Headquarters, he sent for me, and my word didn't he swear at me about my crazy parents. I learnt some swear words that I had never heard before. He showed me the Commanding Officer's letters; all were a lovely shade of pink. Well, the Russian revolution hadn't happened at that stage, but I wonder what people would think getting their letters delivered in a nice shade of pink. He kept himself relatively under control until I foolishly asked him what he had done with the strawberries! Once he had cooled down, we became good friends again as we had been before the incident. He just told me to warn my parents about what they sent to me. No more fruit in cardboard boxes please was his instruction.

Well, the primary purpose of our trip to France was the war, and, on two occasions while we were at Meteren, the Battalion spent twenty-four hours in the line in the sector where we were due to take over. The Commanding Officer said that the signallers weren't required, so we were left behind, much to my relief. Initially, we were upset at being left out of the action; however, another of the signallers reminded me that it was a life and death struggle at the front and we would be better to be safe behind the lines. In fact, it was quite a while, and not until we were losing men at a very high rate that we realised, war was just killing and more killing.

I used to see Fred regularly as being part of the same regiment; we used to bump into each other until he was wounded on the Somme. We used to tell each other about the letters we had received from home. Ethel wrote regularly, and I tried to write as often as I could, even if it was only a field card.

Towards the end of June, we left Meteren and moved nearer to the front line. The noise of the guns firing became a lot louder, and then on June 25^{th,} we moved up to the war area. I still had one of the bicycles, and as we drew nearer to our destination, I dismounted to ensure that I could get lower to the ground. It felt as if the bullets were just going over my head, which they probably were. We arrived at Battalion Headquarters which was a magnificent chateau with a beautiful garden, where lovely flowers still grew. The property stood on the edge of Ploogstreet Wood and was a short distance from Poperings and the Ypres sector. So this is where we spent our first night under fire. War didn't seem to be too bad if this was it; however, at this stage, we didn't know the tragedy that would befall us on the following day.

The next day, June 26th was a Saturday. That morning I went up through the woods to the frontline, which was just the other side of the woods. I saw Fred and my pals in the Platoon, and they all seemed to be in good cheer, Apart from rifle fire, all seemed quiet. No one had seen any Germans, and it was quite a while before they did encounter any. I was reminded to keep my head down as if you raised your head to have a look during daylight hours it meant certain death. Our sentries were using periscopes which were affixed to their rifles. In this way, they were able to scan the territory in front of them. I was told that there were many periscopes that had been shattered by sniper fire while we were in the Armentières section of the front.

After dinner that evening it was my turn to be on duty manning the phones linking Headquarter with the various companies in the area. We already had telephone connections with Brigade HQ, but Sergeant

Dale had picked his team to man the phone that I was on.

The weather had been beautiful and warm in June and some of us signallers had been finding bits of streams etc., where we could have a bath as we were already suffering from body lice. As I mentioned earlier, we were based at a beautiful chateau bordering Ploogstreet Wood, and there was also quite a big garden which was still in good condition and not neglected. Some of the signallers from 'C' Coy were off duty that afternoon, one chap called Mitchell, who came from Norfolk, and one named Jenkins who came from Charing in Kent. Now, these chaps were pals, and they often went paddling and swimming in a large pond at the bottom of the garden. The pond was quite large and was around thirty feet across. That afternoon I was on duty but Mitchell, Jenkins and another signaller from B Coy, went for a swim in the pond. Suddenly, and this is what Robinson told us is what happened, Mitchell, who had stayed in the water longer than the others, got into difficulties. When he shouted for help, Jenkins, who was then partly dressed, pulled off his boots and went to his assistance. Mitchell panicked and grabbed Jenkins and, as neither could swim, they were soon both drowning. Bert Robinson, who was a strong swimmer, jumped in to help. They both grabbed him around the neck and threatened to drown him. He managed to shake himself clear and had to stay away from them as they would have drowned him as well. The Adjutant, Captain Wingfield-Stratford, heard the shouting and ran to see what was going on. He pulled off some of his clothes and dived in. He managed to help Robinson out of the pond. Mitchell and Jenkins had vanished by this stage and had obviously both gone to the bottom of the pond. The locals told us that the pond had a suction which pulled everything to its bottom. We were all shattered, our first day as real soldiers at the front and two of our signallers had been killed, not by the enemy, but in a misadventure. Everyone at Headquarters was very upset at the loss. It took the pioneers, who were attached to Headquarters, a long time to recover the bodies of our good friends, for friends we signallers had become and we were happy together in a tight-knit team. Sergeant Dale was particularly affected by this tragedy. Well, the next day was Sunday, and they arranged for the burial of Mitchell and Jenkins. The pioneers sewed each one up into a blanket and graves were dug in the little cemetery in the wood adjacent to the chateau. Some soldiers who had died in the recent fighting were already resting there; however, these two were the first causalities from our battalion that were laid to rest in France. After breakfast that beautiful Sunday morning, Sergeant Dale called me over to him.

'Kemp, you were a gardener in your civilian life weren't you?'

'Yes Sarge,' I replied.

'Will you please make three wreaths for the guys; you can use the flowers in the garden?'

'I'll do my best Sarge, but I haven't made one before.'

'Well just do your best Kemp.'

My pals made up the frames for the wreaths out of telephone wire. They then stripped some of the wire and gave me thinner pieces to wrap around the flowers. It worked well, and I made good progress. The sergeant ordered me to make three wreaths. One was to be from the Commanding Officer and Adjutant, which I made from Madonna lilies, roses and other suitable flowers. A second one was to be from the Headquarters staff, which included the Regimental Sergeant Major and the signallers. The third one was from Sergeant Dale himself. I felt very proud of my achievement as they all looked very colourful and professional. Although I had helped the head gardener when he made wreaths at Oxon Hoath, I had never done the more difficult bits myself and certainly not while there were shells and bullets flying overhead.

Well, the usual cards were pinned to the wreaths and that Sunday afternoon, with bullets whining overhead, Mitchell and Jenkins were laid to rest in the Ploogstreet Cemetery. Not long in France, but there it was, we had lost two decent chaps who everyone liked. I wonder how many officers and men who fell and were buried in Flanders had real wreaths made for them and placed on their graves. I know that I never made any more wreaths although I did assist in the burial of many of our chaps. Never afterwards did I bathe in streams or ponds, I made myself content with the baths provided by the regiment, or I simply used a bowl.

The section of the line we were going to occupy had been held by the Royal Warwicks, of which Captain Barns' father was an officer. He it was, who later on, gained worldwide fame with his wonderful drawings, especially of 'Old Bill in a better ole'. His sketches were placed on the walls of the dugouts and in the chateau in which our HQ was situated.

After a few days in the line we were relieved, and we went to billets located just across the Belgian border. We rested there and we signallers had to put out telephone lines linking the companies. Sergeant Dale believed in having fully functioning means of communication at all times. I saw Fred regularly, both in the line and when we were out for rest. He usually found plenty to do looking after the equipment etc. of Lieutenant Matthews who was still nagging me to return as a corporal in 8 Platoon.

We had another spell of duty at Ploogstreet Wood. So far we had been fortunate, and we had no casualties. One afternoon I went up to the firing line, and, feeling a bit hateful of the enemy, I blazed away at the German lines with my rifle. When I had finished firing, a German soldier waved a shovel in the air letting me know that I was a waste of space and ammunition. The sergeant in charge of the platoon, based in the trench where I had fired from, swore at me and told me to hop it. He didn't want retaliation he said, which could have been common sense I suppose as we were about to be relieved, or should I say, 'B' Coy were waiting to be relieved, and he didn't want to stir up the enemy. Fred told me that he and others were lying on their backs, with all their equipment on, waiting for the signal to go. Lying beside Fred was a chap called Holman, who came from Ightham. A German whizz-bang arrived in the trench, this was a small shell fired from a canon, and the explosion severed Holman's arm. Fred said that Holman's arm was attached to his body one second and the next it was lying beside him. He was the first serious casualty we had suffered so far, other than Mitchell and

Jenkins. After the war, I met Holman on a few occasions when Ethel and I were living at Crouch.

About the middle of July, arrangements had been put in place so that we went in and out of the line, alternating with the Buffs on a regular basis. Our sector was to the right of Ploogstreet Wood. Our Headquarters, when we were in the line, was at Despiere Farm. We remained in this sector until we left in September to go the battle of Loos.

Sergeant Dale had re-arranged his signallers so he could give an improved service. He asked me to take charge of making sure that the system was working rather than being attached to a station or Headquarters. I had to do a daily check of the whole network that ran through all the company areas, checking the wires for damage and doing the necessary repairs. This routine enabled me to see Fred on a regular basis, and I made a number of good friends in the other companies too.

As the weather was fine and, so far, the war had been gentlemanly, there wasn't a lot of activity. One day I was in the line and a German shell burst close to where I was, the enemy usually sent over whizz bangs on a random basis. They were about the size of our eighteen pounders. When the shell went off a chap, named Rust, was killed. At one point in the line known as the Fort, which was about twenty-five yards from the German line, another chap called Jones was killed. Germany had invented telescopic sights to fit some of their rifles, and this gadget gave them a certain hit if somebody was careless enough to expose their body above the parapet of the trench. I was only standing a few feet away from Rust when he was killed.

Not only did we have our Headquarters, which was located just behind the firing line, but we had a post about half-a-mile further back at a place called Gunner's Farm. This spot was where the General Service waggons came to each evening with our rations etc. We had a signal post at Gunner's Farm. One evening, while the waggons were being unloaded, the Germans started shelling the area. One of our signallers, named Groom, was hit and wounded pretty badly. We heard later that he had a limb amputated at a London hospital. Not only did they hit a signaller, but they also hit the only cow owned by the French couple who were still farming the fields despite them being so close to the trenches. Our wires were also blown to pieces and had to be renewed.

Sergeant Dale gave me a companion, a chap from 'D' Coy by the name of Tommy Atkins. Now Tommy told me one day that he had been Quartermaster on a Canadian ship that had berthed at the London Docks. Wanting to take part in the war, he deserted his ship, found the nearest recruiting office and so joined the Royal West Kent Regiment. One day I said to Tommy; 'What is your real name Tommy?' For some reason, I didn't think that he had given his proper name.

Tommy replied, 'Does it matter; one name is as good as another, isn't it?'

He wasn't going to tell me, so I left it at that.

Tommy never received letters or parcels from home, which he said was in Newfoundland. I don't remember what happened to Tommy afterwards, but, as in so many cases, and some we knew about, fellows enlisted in false names for some reason only known to themselves.

At this time in 1915, the pubs in England and France had carried on as they had done before the war started. They opened at 6.00am in the morning, remaining open all day, often until 11.00pm at night. During the summer of 1915 in France, during the quiet times, it was not unknown for somebody to be despatched from the trenches carrying an empty gallon rum jar in a sandbag to get beer for the Sergeants and men in the line. The journey to the pub happened many times in our Regiment as the Estaminet at Le Touquet, where we were serving was only about a mile from the firing line.

Now about our rations; each man was served independently when in the trenches, for breakfast he had a ration of bread or biscuits and some uncooked bacon. For dinner, he would receive either some raw meat or bully and some jam and tea. For an extended period, it was plum and apple until stocks of that ran out. Then we had tasty jam such as apricot or peach which had been made in Australia. It was a familiar sight on fine mornings to see the smoke from a lot of little fires curling up above the trenches. It was not only on our side but also in the German lines. When men were cooking their breakfast in the lid of their mess tin, they then boiled water in the mess tin itself to make tea, of which each man had his own ration as well as a sugar ration. This method worked fine in dry weather, but men couldn't do the cooking when the rain and mud came to the trenches. In my opinion that was why so many fell sick during the winter of 1915. They just didn't get enough food to eat during the cold and wet months. I know that there was plenty of bully beef; however, eating bully beef morning noon and evening got a bit monotonous, to say the least. I was one of the lucky ones, as, I have said before, my brother Fred was servant to Lieutenant Matthews, and the officers of each company messed together. They also had a cook preparing their meals, even when they were in the trenches. Fred was always able to feed me as well as my two mates who worked on the telephones with me. The phone was always based near to where the officers were billeted in the trenches. I feel sure that I wouldn't have lasted as long as I did if it hadn't been for Fred's help in getting me extra food for us signallers.

At the end of 1915, the chap cooking for the officers in the trenches of 'B' Coy fell sick. Amongst a new draft just joining us was a chap who had been a cook at one of the big London hotels. He was detailed to take over the cooking job. I know that he begged the officers to let him do duty in the trenches as an ordinary foot soldier, but no, they wanted him to cook for them. He said to me: 'Why should I be made to do something that I don't want to do and in such crazy conditions? It's not fair.'

'You haven't got a chance on this one mate; it's the officers' stomachs at risk here, so they won't give in.' I felt that he was right, but the army works by rank, so he had no option.

The officers were very selfish when it came to their food; Lieutenant Matthews was the only one who had any sympathy for the life of a 'ranker'.

When we went back out of the trenches, the cooks were always ready to fill us up. We, at Headquarters, had Nobby and his faults, but even his cooking was acceptable when you were starving. If we hadn't had the tot of rum every evening after stand-to, and in the morning before stand-to, many of us would have broken down in ill-health earlier than we did. We used to get some of the wood used for cooking purposes for making tea, and some of the chaps found broken boxes, etc.

Chapter 7

In the summer of 1915, the sides of the trenches, or to be more accurate I should say the sides of the communication trenches, became covered in poppies. These trenches extended from the front line to the rear for as much as a mile. The farmers could no longer till this land but surprisingly the area was covered in poppies, those lovely red poppies which were a curse to farmers trying to grow corn, I should think that we, the soldiers of Lord Kitchener's new army, were the first people in Flanders to see the poppies blooming. The soldiers of the original BEF, or the ones who were still alive, had been withdrawn and had been taken behind the lines to rest. We had been their replacements. But those immortal men of the original BEF who had landed in France in 1914 had, without any doubt, stopped the German army from taking all of Belgium and France in their original massive attack in August 1914.

Sections of the front line that we shared the defence of together with the Buffs, in some places, were not more than twenty-five yards from the German trenches. On quiet evenings, when I was doing my rounds checking the telephone lines, I could hear a German soldier playing tunes on his accordion. It further emphasised to me how stupid war is.

There was one officer of .B. Coy who was severely wounded during the summer of 1915; his name was Lieutenant Mann. At the time he was hit he was in charge of a working party who were putting up new barbed wire out in front of the line. This type of work was always a dangerous job, especially, for the chap who wielded the sledgehammer to knock in the posts. He had no way of concealing himself while he carried out the task and he often attracted enemy fire. When they heard the noise of the sledgehammer, they used to send up a very light making the area as bright as day. The men caught in the light learnt to stand perfectly still which required a lot of courage; however, if you moved a sniper would get you, and another brave soldier had died. We had German troops from Saxony opposite us for most of the summer, and they liked to talk to us. Although we never saw each other, you would hear the odd shout attracting our attention. They would say things like, 'good morning West Kents,' when we were in the line. We had no idea how they got the information that we were back on the line, but the authorities got worried and instead of using Morse Code to send messages we were told only to use the telephone. There was also a feeling that the Germans were in some way intercepting our telephone messages.

Later on, in 1916, our Royal Engineers developed instruments that were capable of picking up German messages, but more about that later. The Saxon troops were not content in shouting out messages; they also used to make a banner of say six to eight feet long which they could hold on poles above their trenches. They used to tell us such bits of information as how many Russian ships the German fleet had sunk in the Baltic. Well, this amusing practice went on most of the summer.

We received some new weapons during 1915. The first was the Stokes Trench Mortar, another was the Mills hand grenade, and yet another was a rifle grenade which, as its name suggests, was fired in the air from a rifle. Hopefully, the grenade would land in a German trench. The Stokes mortar looked very much like the old mortars seen in military museums, but it could be deadly to the enemy but also to those firing it. As this was a new weapon, some sergeants of 'B' Coy started to practice using it. They brought it to where the trenches were close together and instead of using shells for ammunition they put a tin of bully beef in the barrel. They put the charge in and aimed to send the tin of bully beef into the German trench. Our fellows were very successful at doing this, and each time a can landed in the German trench the Germans cheered. On our right, another regiment did the same manoeuvre, but one of their tins of bully beef fell short of the German trench where it lay, just out of reach. A German soldier crawled out of the trench to retrieve it and when he climbed down some fool let a shot off at him probably killing the poor fellow. Such behaviour wasn't playing the game as our guys saw it and they were very upset. We were always afraid of upsetting the enemy in case they increased the shelling.

We didn't have long to wait. About twenty-four hours later the Germans sent their reply. They moved up heavy Howitzer guns and blasted the Regiment who had carried out the unfair deed, and they also bombarded the West Kents. As many men as possible bolted away from where the shells were falling, but our trench, as I saw later, was a complete shambles. We also had a few casualties but didn't learn whether the other regiment had any. Well, of course, there was an inquiry about this sudden vicious arrack by the Germans, who, before this incident, were trying to be friendlier than other Germans that we had encountered. The outcome of it all, and this came out as a Battalion order, was that at no time anywhere are British troops to speak to or fraternise with the enemy. So, a period, when two peoples of the human race had been able to communicate with one another, came to an end.

When we used to go from this part of the line to our rest area at Touquet, we, of the Battalion Headquarters used to stay in part of a chateau. The Commanding Officer and his staff used to stay in the other part. Adjoining the grounds was a nice flat area of meadow land. The weather was beautiful, and someone had got hold of some cricket gear, so the signallers were able to have several games of cricket amongst ourselves. The cricket came to an end when we came back from our period in the trenches and found that the Germans had been using our field for target practice and it was now full of shell holes and not suitable to play cricket on. Also, until the trouble with the bully beef cans, we and the Buffs used to march up the road leading to the front line in say half Coys, and we had never been fired on. One day when the Buffs were marching forward to relieve us, the Germans suddenly opened fire on them. They were helpless as there was no cover. Some were killed, and quite a lot were wounded. After that incident, we used to relieve each other in small parties and at irregular times. I feel now as I did then, why didn't that stupid Tommy just let the Jerry take the tin of Bully Beef which would have prevented all the reprisals. I supposed the person who did the shooting believed that there was a war on and he was meant to kill the enemy. That is the question I have been asking myself for over fifty years, and I still don't have the correct answer. Just being humane to one another is probably the answer.

After we had landed in France, we were told that all our letters would be censored except for ones that we wrote and then sealed in a green envelope that we were issued with. On the back of this envelope was a declaration stating that there were no military secrets etc. inside and we then signed it with our names. The censoring of letters caused a lot of dissent amongst the chaps. Their attitude was that they didn't object to censors at the base or elsewhere reading their letters, but they did object to their own platoon officers reading what they wrote to wives, sweethearts and parents. Unfortunately, some of the officers took great delight in reading the letters right through. Fred used to give me his green envelope and any others that he could scrounge, so I was able to write pretty frequently to Ethel without a nosy Lieutenant reading it and making remarks about what I had written. One officer, who was attached to the Intelligence section of Headquarters, loved to read the letters we sent to our parents. He remarked to me, in front of my colleagues, hadn't I anything better to write to my parents than how close I had been to an exploding shell when my friend was killed. He clearly liked to read our letters for his own sadistic pleasure.

Our Lieutenant Matthews, my brother told me, hardly glanced at fellows' letters before he sealed and initialled them. There were many other irritating things that needed attention, and if sorted, would have helped us immensely. For instance; for weeks on end, we never had a bath, and we also had to wear our shirts for long periods. I used to wash my shirt when we were out of the line and went around without a shirt until it was dry. We were becoming 'licy', and it was not unusual to see a chap in the trenches with his shirt off, running a lighted candle up and down the seams to try and get rid of the lice and nits. Rats were also becoming plentiful in the trenches, and you didn't dare leave any food around. All spare food had to be kept in your mess tin or hung up where the rats couldn't get it. It seemed as if war brings out the bad things in nature. Where did those huge rats come from and I mean that they were as big as cats? I can't believe that the French farmers allowed them to live around their farms before the war.

Nothing much changed for the rest of July. The Germans were shelling us a lot more frequently now, and our artillery would retaliate. Although the shelling was more frequent, it still was not like we had to endure at a later date. During the summer of 1915, there was a small biplane which was kept behind our lines and used by a chap who we called the 'Mad Major'. We saw him on a number of occasions. He was a heavily built tall man, very large for the size of the plane he was flying. He used to take his little plane over the German lines, and loop the loop again and again. It used to drive the Germans crazy, and they opened up on him with their anti-aircraft guns, but all he would do was dance away from the exploding shells. They used to fire as many as two hundred shells at him, but he was just able to keep in front of the bursting shells. It was great for our morale. We never saw a German pilot do the same and I am glad to relate that the Mad Major survived the war.

Before we left Aldershot for France, word was passed around that if anyone wished to make an allotment from their pay when they went overseas, they could do so. I spoke to Fred, and we agreed to make an allotment to our parents to pay for parcels, etc. that they would send us. The minimum amount that we agreed to was six pence per day which meant that out of our seven shillings per week we were allotting half to our parents. Before the allotment could be sanctioned, an investigator would have to call and sign them off as genuine. Given the fact, Fred and I were both fighting in France, and there was nobody to help them run the farm, they were approved as genuine. In fact, they were authorised to receive ten shillings over and above the allotment we had signed over to them. Many fellows did the same; we were only trying to help. In hindsight, when I went home for Christmas in 1914 Ethel and I should have got married on what was called a soldier's licence for marriage. In that case, Ethel would have drawn her wife's allowance and would probably have gone to live with my parents and helped out on the farm. It was only when I was invalided out of the army in 1917 that we were happily married. When I asked her why she hadn't suggested that we got married at Christmas 1914, she said that it wasn't right for her to ask me. Still, we had fifty-two years of happily married life together from early 1918 until May 1970.

We were paid five francs per week in France. A franc, when we first arrived in the country, was worth nine pence in English money. I had always had enough money to spend. I didn't gamble or go to the estaminets. My main objective was to remain alive and be able to return to Kent and marry my beloved Ethel. As a token of my love, I used to send Ethel the silk cards.

Towards the end of July, we were doing six days in the line and six out; alternating with the Buffs. Some officer got the bright idea that we ought to tidy up the trenches and keep them a lot cleaner. All of us servants, including the signallers, were sent forward carrying duckboards and other bits and pieces to smarten them up. In fact, our part looked really good when we had finished. Near the end, the whole platoon was helping.

I mentioned earlier that I rode a bicycle when we went into the line; however, they decided that it was too dangerous for signallers to ride bikes. Only one chap from each company was stationed at Battalion Headquarters with the signallers to act as runners. If communications broke down because of a breakage in the telephone cable between Brigade HQ or in the lines connecting the companies, the runners had to get the messages through – a pretty dangerous job it was too. One runner from HQ, when we were on the Somme, was sent out with a message for the front line and was never seen again. He was most likely blown to pieces by a shell. The Companies also had two runners each to provide communication between the Company Commander and Battalion HQ when their telephone lines were broken.

One of the chaps in 'B' Coy was named Bob Smith, and he came from Sevenoaks. Bob wasn't very big but wasn't he tough and fearless. I used to wonder when we were in the line together and he had to take the Company Commander's bag to Battalion HQ, how he managed not to be afraid. Many of the fellows, who lived in a town back in England, were scared of being alone in the depth of the night. Fred and I had lived in a pretty wild part of Kent at our parents' home. We were used to the wind howling in the trees, owls hooting and foxes barking. Bob came from the large town of Sevenoaks which would have been a lot more civilised. After the war when I moved with my employer Mr and Mrs Constant who had appointed me head gardener, I bumped into Bob and found out where he was living. In fact, he lived in a bit of a wild place close to the Tonbridge Road, behind the White Heart Hotel, in amongst a lot of trees and shrubbery. Like Fred and I he must have grown up hearing the noises of the countryside. I met Bob many times after we moved to Sevenoaks and am sorry to say that he died a few years ago. He was awarded the Military Medal for his bravery near the end of the war, and I feel that he richly deserved it as he kept going right up to Armistice Day.

Now back to Le Touquet and the trenches. Let me explain about the trenches; they were not just trenches dug down as you see for roadworks around the UK. The trench was roughly three or four feet below ground level. The soil was then heaped up in front to form a firing step, which the chaps stood on when they were firing their rifles. The trench had to be wide enough to be able to get a stretcher through, and at the back of the trench, dugouts were made with timber structures and galvanised sheets for roofs. Soil, often in sand bags, was heaped on top and around these dugouts and that was home while you were in the line on trench duty. If the Germans shelled our trenches, as they were starting to do more often by the end of July, then the working parties had to repair the damage as quickly as possible. Of course, we had a lot of barbed wire out in front and yet, both we, the British and the Germans, often managed to get through it. We had to keep cheerful and overcome the terrible conditions.

When the rains came, everyone was pretty miserable. It was impossible to brew a cup of tea or to fry the bacon, and it was just biscuits and bully-beef and a drink of water for dinner and tea. In the British trenches at Le Touquet, metal plates had been inserted in the side of the parapet facing the Germans, for it was certain death if you put your head up to sight a rifle from the parapet in day-time. You could do that at night when it was dark, but obviously, you couldn't take a bead on a German at night. Now in the middle of those plates, and there were only a few available in each trench, there was a slide that left just enough space for a chap to put his rifle barrel through and get a sight on the enemy. One day, a chap from 'C' Coy. I forget his name now, but his parents were the landlords of a public house in Week Street, Maidstone, opposite the Royal West Kent barracks. Anyway, he opened the slot in the plate to have a look before putting his rifle through, and he was shot dead by a sniper. The sniper almost certainly had a rifle fitted with a telescopic sight. Another chap from 'D' Coy, by the name of Smith, had a German bullet go right up into the barrel of his rifle before exploding as it got to the breech. I knew this chap, as I knew the other one, as my duties repairing the signal wire took me amongst the chaps every day. Now Smith's rifle was brought to Battalion HQ where the armourer sergeant, who was allocated to each Battalion in case of rifle trouble, examined it and showed the remarkable sight to all the officers at HQ. They couldn't believe that so much damage could be done to the breech of a rifle and still, the user wasn't injured. We were told later that the damaged gun was sent to the Royal West Kent Depot at Maidstone and it is now one of the exhibits at the Royal West Kent section of the Maidstone Museum in Earl Street. About six years ago the Royal West Kent trustees tried to locate Private Smith, but to all the appeals there was no answer, he apparently didn't exist. Most likely he was soldiering under an assumed name like Tommy Atkins was.

Chapter 8

As July moved into August, the German artillery became more active which increased the amount of work that Tommy and I had to do. Not only did we have to repair our own wires, but we also had to repair the red wires belonging to the artillery. Another of our group of signallers was badly wounded near the Fort. The Germans dropped a shell on a dug-out causing severe causalities, one of these was my pal from Dunton Green, named George Collins. His body was covered in small wounds caused by shrapnel when the shell burst. In some ways, he was lucky as he was transferred back to Blighty and he was then invalided out of the army. His war was over, and he survived. I met him again soon after Ethel, and I moved to Sevenoaks, and he told me that he still had bits of shrapnel in his body. Unfortunately, he died many years ago.

August 4th arrived, so the war had now been on for a year. Those who had said that the war would be over by Christmas had been proved very wrong. We were out of the line resting and, for a change; we marched to Pont de Nieppe, where we were able to have a lovely bath. This was the first real bath that I had since leaving England. Fred and I were getting parcels on a regular basis from our parents, Ethel and a Mr and Mrs Pomfret, who were close friends of the family. For the first two weeks of August, we were in the line for six days at a time, coming out for rest and then going back as working parties to help repair and enhance the walls of the trenches which the Germans kept knocking down with their shelling.

Behind the German lines was a tall chimney which our officers said the Germans were using as an observation point. Our artillery, which all through the war was noted for its accuracy in shooting, took a few shots to establish the range and it was not long before the chimney was a mass of broken rubble. This type of activity kept our minds occupied as it was something out of the mundane day to day situation.

About the middle of August, we started getting thunderstorms; some were pretty severe. We soon found out how difficult life could be living out in the open as we were. On August 18th we were out of the line, and we were told to smarten ourselves up as that afternoon we were to represent the 12th Division "Ace of Spades" at a parade. It was going to be on the Nieppe Road where we would be inspected by Lord Kitchener, the War Minister. His lordship walked down our ranks, and the whole of the battalion was on parade. Afterwards, he congratulated our Commanding Officer and the Adjutant for our soldier-like manner. Lord Kitchener was a huge man, in fact, he was the biggest man I had ever seen, and his medal ribbons on his chest seemed to be in the dozens. He appeared to be a man who you could serve under, and I was told that he knew his job. I have always wondered why the powers that be kept Lord Kitchener away from France and still thought that they could win the war. In the end, it was a soldier from France, Marshal Foch, who brought final victory to the allies. We were one of Lord Kitchener's first divisions to go overseas, and I feel that he was pleased that we were conducting ourselves as soldiers should.

It was in August that the Divisional Command formed teams to fire trench mortar guns. These new mortars were bigger than the ones that had fired the bully beef tins over to the Germans. They fired a shell about the size of an eighteen pounder which was what our small field guns were firing. I was detailed on several occasions, to lay wires to these gunners in the trenches from our Battalion HQ. I made sure that I got well away from where they were situated before they commenced firing as did most of the rest of the infantry. Once they had fired four or five shells, the gunners then disappeared as fast as they could down the communication trench. Jerry would then retaliate; we started calling the enemy Jerry about this time, up to now they had been called Huns. It was like a game but a dangerous one. Their artillery, we found out, also used trench mortars and didn't they make a mess of the trenches. With careful aiming, they were able to get the shell to fall and burst right in the trench.

Small parties were also now being trained in the use of the Mills hand grenade. This new grenade was about the size of a lemon and chaps became skilled in knowing how long to hold the bomb before throwing it into the German lines. If the grenade was thrown too soon, then the Germans could lob it back at us. There were a few accidents when they were first used, but soon the chaps became experts, especially those who had played cricket before the war.

Another interesting fact was that everybody got on well, there were never any quarrels. The fellows had come from all walks of life, some rich, some poor, some middle class and some working class. It seemed as if the common purpose was for everyone to try and get the job done and also to survive. But there was plenty of swearing, the good old British words such as bloody, etc. were part of everyday language. Some used the more refined phrases, but I feel this is not the place to air them. Later on, in 1916, I met a chap called Charlie Moon whose home was in Southborough near the Wells. He became a corporal and was transferred from 'D' Coy to 'B' Coy. I think that Charlie was the most God-fearing Christian chap that I met during my time with the army. He wasn't a bible bashing nut-case but was just an honest, good living Christian gentleman. Charlie used to rebuke me for swearing. He used to say to me, 'Sid, you are one of the nicest chaps that I have ever met; but please do not swear so.'

Later on, Charlie was recommended for the Victoria Cross but died not knowing if it had actually been awarded to him. But more about Charlie later.

August 24th was the anniversary of the day on which Fred and me, plus our other friends from the area, enlisted at Maidstone Barracks. We were still doing line duty at Le Touquet, alternating with the Buffs. Before we were relieved that day, our chaps had been heavily shelled by the German artillery. We had several casualties, but fortunately, none killed. So far in the trenches, we had several casualties; however, no officer had been killed, and only Lieutenant Mann had been wounded. I met my brother, Fred, as we always used to meet when we were relieved, and I also met him and talked to him when I was doing my inspection and repair of the telephone lines. In our battalion were several pairs of brothers and I knew at least three other pairs besides

Fred and I. The practice of having brothers serve together in a Battalion was stopped after a while as families lost all their sons when they went into action together.

It was on August 28th that we of the Royal West Kents, who were out of the line, were told that there would be an inspection by the Officer Commanding the Second Army, General Plumer. The inspection would take place that afternoon at the same location as last time on the Nieppe Road. General Plumer, like Lord Kitchener, had been very successful in the South African war at the turn of the century. Unlike Lord Kitchener, Plumer was a much shorter, thick-set man, but he looked what he was, a fine General. He too had many ribbons decorating his left breast.

Well, he too was very pleased with our appearance, and this was noted in the Battalion orders. It was another confirmation that the new Battalions were maturing and becoming more like regular soldiers.

The weather was getting much cooler now, with a lot of continuous rain at times, but we hadn't yet met the full force of the severe weather conditions which would thin our ranks so considerably.

We now were able to have baths on a regular basis when we went out of the line. We were still troubled with lice, which appeared to be coming out of the ground. Sometimes, if you lay on your back on the ground, you would find the outside of your clothes covered with lice and these didn't seem to be the same as the body lice. Body lice were white in colour, but these others were much darker.

We continued our routine with the Buffs of six days in and six days out. There were plenty of working parties now, including the signallers and servants. The aim was to make them model trenches; however, the Germans had other ideas. They kept up the bombardment of the communication trenches, and we had several more casualties. Tommy and I were kept busy mending and laying new wires, not only to the forward companies but also for the artillery.

September arrived, and we continued our alternating pattern with the Buffs. The weather was very mixed, but there still was quite a lot of rain to inconvenience us. We kept to our established routine and didn't think too much about the future.

All of us knew that the war wouldn't be won by either side if we kept on going as we were, for clearly there was a stalemate. We were resigned to be fighting a war for the foreseeable future which wasn't a very exciting prospect.

We didn't have much longer to wait before we knew that somebody in high places was making a plan to try and end it all by breaking the stalemate.

We continued to get letters and parcels from home and other friends that cared about us. Ethel, God bless her, wrote regularly to me and I wrote back to her when I got a chance. I used the green envelopes whenever possible to make sure that my officers didn't read the personal things that I was writing.

It was while we were serving in this sector of the line that the armourer's assistant, a chap named Sales who came from Dunton Green, near Sevenoaks, spotted a Hare in the land between the Jerry trenches and our reserve trench. He was returning to Battalion HQ after delivering a repaired rifle to the owner. He shot the hare but was then too scared to go and fetch it. But what good would it have been to any of us as our cooks would have had no idea how to cook it. The Hare probably ended up providing dinners for a family of rats. I myself never saw any wild animals; no rabbits or the like and there were no wild birds, not even behind the battle zones. Back in England, there were always those friendly sparrows plus other birds flitting around. Was it the war or the shelling that caused the absence of birds? But never do I remember seeing wild birds when we were at rest ten or twelve miles behind the lines. Another reason for the lack of birds may have been the fact that over the years the people of Belgium and France, in this part of the world, had removed all the hedgerows and small coppices and cultivated the fields, right up to the roads. There was nowhere for the birds to nest. In Britain, in those days, the fields were surrounded by hedgerows where the birds could nest and rear their young. I feel that this is something that should be recorded; that there were no birds anywhere; no rooks, no crows, no starlings or thrushes, no blackbirds and no robins.

It was on September 23rd that we were given a job of bundling up straw, for what purpose we weren't told. The artillery to the left of us at the battlefield of Ypres was busy. To the South, the artillery was also firing. They were bombarding the Germans day and night in a fearsome barrage. We were all wondering what was afoot. It was about this time that I again met Len Bush who I had met previously when I was home on leave from Sandling Junction over Christmas in December 1914. Len, with his regiment, for he was a regular soldier, had been sent to France when he returned from four years' service in India. He was in the 2nd Battalion of the Buffs and was also engaged to Ethel's eldest sister Flo, who was about my age. He had been wounded at the end of March 1915 and had now returned to serve with the 6th Buffs who were our sister regiment in France and who were doing alternate duty with us. He was able to tell me that our artillery had been withdrawn from the Armentières front and we were now covered by other artillery. On September 22nd the Commanding Officer inspected the Battalion on parade, and we were then taken to do duty at Divisional HQ at Nieppe. We began to wonder what was going on; there was a general feeling that something was afoot. There seemed to be a greater purpose in what we were being asked to do, and we seemed to be preparing for something big.

Reflections - Chapters 5 to 8

In the last four chapters, Sid tells us about the excellent Hospitals and Nursing Homes that were established to care for the war wounded. If you once made it back to 'Blighty', and that was quite an ordeal in itself, you had a much greater chance of survival and conditions were reasonable. Volunteers from cities in other countries, such as Boston in the USA, supplied the hospital staff for some of the hospitals required to treat so many wounded and sick. A nice touch was the local Council allowing the recovering wounded to ride on the trams for free etc. it was really appreciated by the wounded men. It made them feel that they were appreciated. Depending on where you were recovering there were other free perks on offer for the recovering wounded; such as Cinema, Theatre and concerts.

When Sid was recovering from his sickness in Brighton, he saw many severely maimed and wounded soldiers who were in various establishments around the town. He speaks for a lot of his colleagues when he says, 'why couldn't the politicians see what their decision to wage war was doing to the young men of England'. Surely a disagreement between two or three countries could be resolved before any more men ended up being destroyed. The simple fact was that the politicians, on both sides, had started something that they didn't know how to stop.

Let's now reflect on Sid Kemp's daily existence at the front in France.

He and the other signallers had a lot of respect for Sergeant Dale who had come out of retirement and re-enlisted in 1914. He was a seasoned soldier who had served in South Africa and other places. He just got on with his job in a fair and professional manner. It was people like him who were involved in training Kitchener's Army and who looked after the key men when they went to France. The men also had great respect for the experienced officers who re-enlisted. Sadly most of those experienced officers didn't survive the war, including my grandfather.

When Sid arrived in France, he describes the war as being 'sort of gentlemanly'. By the time his Battalion arrived, both sides were entrenched, and the mobile war had ceased. Not much was going on. The Germans were consolidating their defensive positions while the French and English were making sure that the enemy stayed in their trenches and didn't move into other parts of France. Neither side enjoyed being there but just got on with life the best that they could. The time provided by this stalemate was used by the British to organise factories back in England to manufacture all the items required for the war. Gradually the availability of shells and other essentials improved although there were still hurdles to overcome and there were significant ordinance shortages at times.

The system that the allies had developed to keep the troops supplied with food worked in the summer months. Once it started to rain and get cold, then the men went hungry. The Officers were alright as they had a chef or cook providing them with food. The men in the trenches had to cook over a small kerosene stove using their billy can. In cold and wet weather they couldn't use this method, so the men got hungry and as a consequence got sick. They did have plenty of bully beef and biscuits, but they preferred to go hungry rather than have these two items for every meal.

One process that worked extremely well was the postal service. The front line troops were able to keep in touch with their loved ones at home, and the time taken for a letter to travel in either direction wasn't more than a few days. Various packages could also be sent such as food products. Sid relates an amusing delivery he had of some fresh strawberries which had turned to mush by the time they reached the postman delivering to his Battalion Headquarters, where he was based. The officers' and Battalion letters were all a sticky pink as a result of the rogue package of strawberries.

There is mention of the Germans having a lot of snipers with telescopic sights. The British had snipers, and they also had telescopic sights, but they were in very short supply as they were very expensive and they weren't as good.

The Germans made an art form out of sniping and killed a lot more of the enemy that way. Also, the German snipers were not attached to any particular Regiment so when the German regiments moved in and out of an area of the front; the snipers didn't move with them. This method of operation gave them a chance to become very familiar with the territory they were operating in. By staying in the same place, they got to know exactly where the best place to find a victim was. The allies never used snipers to their best effect, mainly because they moved when their units moved, so they were always familiarising themselves with a new territory. One wonders why the allies didn't change the modus operandi for the snipers to make them more effective.

Sid relates the first time that he saw significant numbers of red Poppies. It must have been a magnificent sight when they first appeared on the side of the communication trenches and in other parts of No-Man's Land,

The whole issue of secrecy in World War 1 is a very contentious one. The powers that be were very keen on censoring the letters being sent home from the front-line troops, but they didn't spend enough time trying to discover how the Germans were always aware of what was going on. Captured British Officers were often carrying written details of the offensive that they were involved in, including the timing of follow-up attacks. Even troops being captured and then being interrogated were giving away crucial information. It has been said that they were so relieved to have survived and be captured that they didn't see anything wrong in telling their captors what was going on. They reckoned that they would be better treated if they passed on useful information.

If semaphore was used for communication, then the Germans could read the message that was being relayed. It was also found that the Germans were able to listen to messages being sent over the allied telephone lines and were able to interpret the messages. The British also developed this technique a little bit later in the war. It is fair to say that enough time and effort was not spent in making sure that the enemy didn't get forewarning of the British offensives. It took far too long to realise the importance of secrecy and to develop a secure system to protect critical information. It was obviously essential to stop the Germans knowing what the allies' plans were and the exact time when they were going to start an offensive. With the information that they obtained, the Germans were able to set up their defensive strategy and especially place their machine guns where they would do the most damage.

One event that cheered the troops up no-end was the arrival of new armaments at the front, but it does appear that they were used before a satisfactory methodology was arrived at or before the men were trained in how to use them.

The Mills Grenade became one of the best weapons of the war and gave them a means of attacking machine gun nests. It is interesting to note that men who had played cricket were the most accurate throwers of the grenade.

As the war progressed, the amount of work that Sid Kemp and the team of Signallers had to do increased considerably. The more the Germans shelled the communication trenches, the more times the wires were cut, and contact lost. Of course, it was essential that the break in the wire was found and repaired as quickly as possible. The more he was forced to move around the trenches, the greater was the risk of Sid being hit, and quite a few of his fellow signallers were lost. As they were carrying out their duties, they also had to repair the red wire that was used by the artillery. This red line was used to connect the guns with the command centre. The phones used by the infantry were linked by black wire. They often found it saved a lot of time if they ran a new cable, rather than to try and locate the break in the existing one.

It is also interesting to read that the men at the front had great respect for Lord Kitchener and felt that he should have been in charge rather than General French and later Field Marshal Haig. They believed that Kitchener wouldn't have made the same number of mistakes that the existing Generals had made as he appeared to know what he was doing. The feeling amongst the troops was that only Kitchener was capable of winning the war in the short term. This possibility was taken off the list when the Field Marshal was lost at sea in 1916 on his way to a meeting in Russia.

Chapter 9

On September 25th, 1915, it seemed as if all hell had been let loose by the British Artillery to the left and the right of us, and it appeared to cover quite a distance to the right of us. We learned later that the barrage was the start of the Loos offensive on September 25th. The shelling was the start of the big breakthrough we all sensed was coming. We learnt later that there was no breakthrough, and, in fact, the amount of ground gained was very small. For such a miniscule amount of gains, there had been a massive loss of life.

The rest of the 12th Division had been withdrawn from the Armentières sector to support the Loos attack. The whole of our section of the line was now being held, oh so lightly, by the 6th Buffs, who were spread out across the front in small groups of two or three men. This part of the line had, up until very recently, been held by six battalions each with a reserve Battalion. We, the Royal West Kents, were still in reserve to the Buffs. They were issued with the straw that we had previously bundled up. They were told to light it and create masses of smoke. The wind was blowing from behind our lines, so the smoke wafted over the German trenches. It was supposed to cause panic amongst the Jerrys. It was this German Regiment who had used gas against the Canadians at Ypres earlier in the year. Len Bush, who was now with the Buffs told me later; they lit the straw, the smoke drifted across the German trenches, and the Germans climbed onto the parapet begging our fellows, who were the Buffs, to take them, prisoner. The Buffs were so thinly spread over the front that they could do nothing, as the number of Germans wanting to be taken prisoner far exceeded the number of men they had in the line. If the High Command had been on their toes, they could have switched that night's attack to our part of the line, and they could have had their breakthrough. Of course, our commanders had no idea what was going on as they very seldom came near the front once the attacks started. The idea of the smoke was a good idea, but there was no plan in place to take advantage of it.

Well, we could hear the attack going on at Loos and couldn't understand why we were messing around where we were, that is the Buffs and us. We learned later that we were waiting for the second contingent of the Canadian Army to relieve us. We would then be able to take part in the Loos attack, which had already started. The Canadians hadn't arrived, so we were unable to take up our vital role in the van of the Loos attack. It wasn't until the night of September 27th, two days later, when we were all off the roads, waiting in the fields, that the Canadians marched up to take their positions relieving the Buffs. We heard later that they hadn't even left Shorncliffe, near Folkestone, when the battle of Loos had begun on September 25th. On arrival, they then needed time to familiarise themselves with the area and take over from the Buffs. Having just left England, it was all new to them. Both the Buffs and the West Kents then marched to Armentières station where trains had been waiting for several days to take us to the battle that was now over three days old.

It was on September 29th that we finally moved off by train and travelled by Steinwert back to Hazebrouck, which was a junction. We were then offloaded at a little station a few miles from Bethune. The entire complement of two battalions had to be accommodated in a small village, and, as the nights were getting a lot colder, the Quartermasters of both regiments thought that they had housed everybody, but, they had forgotten the signallers and runners of the Kents. There was nowhere for us to sleep until a French farmer, whose house our CO and his staff were using, offered to move his cows out of the cow shed so as we could sleep where the cows were now lying. We helped him muck the area out and put fresh straw down for us to sleep on. Eventually, we were able to sleep. After a night's rest at this little village called Vandrecourt, we marched a bit nearer to the battle which was still raging just down the line. Before we left Vandrecourt, we were told that this would be a forced march as we were required as reserves for another Division. The three miles an hour with five minutes rest wouldn't happen; we would have to go quicker. The signallers, who marched in front of the Battalion, didn't feel it too much, but the company at the rear, after we had marched for several miles, began to suffer. Men couldn't keep up the pace and were starting to collapse and stagger along. The doctor, of which every battalion had one, was an Irishman named Doctor Gordon. He rode a Cob and kept approaching the CO to ask him to halt for a few minutes so as the rear company could get to the front and the company at the front could go to the rear. This was the practice used when we marched at a normal pace as it shared the role of being the last company in the column. I heard the CO tell the doctor that his orders were not to stop until they reached their destination, which as far as I can remember was a distance of around ten miles. At last the doctor rode up and told the CO; 'Sir, I am the doctor of this Battalion, and in the name of humanity I order you to halt this column, if only for five minutes.' The CO gave the order to halt.

He wasn't in luck; thirty yards or so in front of where we had halted the Brigadier of 37th Brigade, of which we were a part, rode out onto the road. He swore and carried on at our Commanding Officer. He and his Aide de Camp had been hiding behind some trees in a little cul de sac. The doctor, who was liked and respected by everyone, rode his pony up to the old Brigadier, saluted and said to him; 'Sir it was I who halted this column and it was not the Commanding Officer.' The Brigadier muttered something and said, 'don't waste too much time they need your men.' He then rode off. Now, this all happened a few feet from where we signallers were resting beside the road, and I know that it happened as all I have written in this story happened to my knowledge, and nothing is hearsay.

We finally reached our objective, which was Vermelles. We immediately went into reserve to the 1st Division who were currently attacking the German positions. We were told later that we should have been there to take part in the assault on the first day of the offensive, September 25th. As I mentioned previously the reason that we were so late was because the Canadians hadn't arrived at Armentières; nobody appeared to have worked through the logistics of the operation which seemed extraordinary to us simple Tommies.

We were also told that the 24th Division, of which the 8th Battalion Royal West Kents were a part, had been marching up to the area from base, having recently arrived from England. When we didn't arrive, they were thrown into the battle in our place. Chaps, who up to that point had never been in the trenches or seen the horrors of war, had to start fighting immediately in a major offensive I heard that a chap called Harmsworth, from Borough Green, had been severely wounded and the losses the battalion suffered were terrible. The Commanding Officer was also killed. Why didn't those in command learn to play chess or even a game of draughts so as they could organise what was going on? From where we were it looked very simple, and the commanders had totally screwed up. Of course, you couldn't say anything, or you would be branded a rebel and probably shot.

We were billeted in houses that were heavily damaged by shells. We slept downstairs as the upstairs had been blown off by the shelling. I was detailed to accompany Lieutenant Harris, who at this time was Intelligence Officer, to scout out the positions that our battalion was to take up the following day. At the last minute, that idea was cancelled and instead we were moved back to another village to rest.

Now let me go back a bit. While we were in the Armentières sector, we were issued with our first gas mask. This mask consisted of a piece of gauze covered by a kind of cotton material with two strings so that we could tie the contraption over our mouth and nose. It was then tied behind our ears. There was no way that this contraption could be worn for many minutes at a time as it severely restricted our breathing. This description of the mask is the preamble to what I about am to tell you.

We stayed in reserve at Vermelles until October 3rd, my brother's birthday; he was twenty-one. We marched back to a small town called Magingarbe which was the HQ of the Guards. When the Royal West Kents arrived, the place was full of troops. While we, the Headquarters staff, under the command of the Regimental Sergeant Major were waiting on the street to go into our billets, the RSM suddenly called us to attention and saluted an officer who was walking on his own down the street. When the officer had passed, the RSM told us that the man was His Royal Highness, the Prince of Wales, who at that time was an officer in one of the Grenadier Guards battalions. About four or five minutes later, the Germans dropped a huge shell, called a coal box because of the dense black smoke it produced on exploding, right into the street where His Royal Highness had just been.

The Prince wasn't hurt, but our Lewis Machine Gun Crew, who were waiting a bit down the street from where I was, were badly injured or killed. Guardsmen later told us that the Prince did his spell of duty in the line in the same way that the other officers did, and he was a Captain, in charge of a company. One chap named Private Page, who died that day, I knew personally. He had been in 8 Platoon with me, and his home was at West Farleigh near Maidstone. Also, young Mitchley was badly injured by another shell that fell in the village.

On October 5th, we left Magingarbe to march back to the front. Terrific shelling was going on by both sides as we neared Vermelles, for the main road passed through this village to go to Hulloch, Loos and Lens and the other battlegrounds further East. This is where the war really started for our Battalion. Let me say that Vermelles was a street with rows of small houses some in terraces etc. with shops on both sides of the main street. Now to the east of Vermelles, and I am pretty certain about this, there were very few trees, no hedges and no buildings. You could see a distance up the valley of about half-a-mile, and it was a further half-a-mile before we came to the first captured German trench which ran parallel with the road leading from Vermelles to Hulloch and beyond. I was always able to judge distances fairly accurately.

In the area that we had to go through there were sights that shocked us and sickened us too. The ground was literally covered by the bodies of Scottish soldiers lying in all grotesque positions. Some facing the Germans, some facing left and some facing right. These dead men were all wearing kilts. It looked terrible for not only were they swollen to two or three times their normal size, but their faces and hands were black as coal. The answer to this was gas, not German gas as was used earlier at Ypres, but British gas. These brave young men from Scotland had just rushed hell for leather into the gas that they were supposed to be following. Our second in command of 'B' Coy, Captain Towse, begged to be allowed to take his company and bury these chaps. To put it mildly, I should say that there were hundreds of the flower of Scotland lying there, dead. We later found out that two Scottish Divisions, the 9th and the 15th were thrown into the battle and very few of them survived. They were the same as us; they had all volunteered and ended up being slaughtered in gaining only a few German trenches. None of the soldiers we saw there was wearing a gas mask or respirator or whatever you call it, simply because it was impossible to go on a bayonet charge wearing the mask as you weren't able to breathe. The mistake they made was to travel in the cloud of gas and not simply follow it. The sight that we saw that day still haunts me.

After the war, when Ethel and I had moved to Sevenoaks, we met a Scottish lady named Mrs Stott who was a Campbell by birth. She told us that almost every family in Scotland lost a family member that day, bereaved by the tragedy of that gas attack which was a total failure. It was part of the battle of Loos in September 1915.

We were now occupying the captured German trenches, and these were very few in number. The Hohenzollern Redoubt, of which the battle of Loos seemed to be about, was a vast honeycomb of fortified trenches, each one a fortress of its own. Even the communication trenches had been constructed so as soldiers could fire from them. Moving up this road to Hulloch, we saw a sight the like of which I luckily never saw again. There was a British infantryman and a German soldier standing leaning against one another. Both had lunged at the same time with their bayonets, and each bayonet was right through the body of the other killing them both instantly. This event happened, no doubt, on the first day of the battle, September 25th, and these chaps, enemies to one another, had died very close to each other. It was pretty horrible to see, but this is what real war was. What we had been doing earlier in the Armentières' sector was just playing at war; that is how I saw it, and I still do.

Chapter 10

Having lost some of their key defences, the Germans were upset and started to counter attack in a big way. They must have brought up many more guns for their bombardment went on for hours at a time. Our battalion was divided up amongst the captured German trenches. 'C' and 'D' Coy were together in one trench, and 'A' and 'B' Coy were in another together with our Commanding Officer. Headquarters were tucked in beside a Guards regiment; I think it was the Coldstream Guards.

One of the trenches had only been partly captured in the attack, so it was vital, to both sides, to capture the rest of it. It was called Gun Trench; it was to the right of our Headquarters. I never understood how or why this fortified area had been created in such detail by the Germans, but the most fortified part was situated at the end of the bit of trench that I was in. There was a major problem in getting water and rations up to people occupying that area. We couldn't use water to wash, and we couldn't even make a brew of tea. The parties who went to the rear to get food and water never returned to the trench. They were most likely victims of the intense German bombardment that stretched well behind into the reserve line and beyond. I didn't have a cup of tea or any other warm drink or food for at least ten days, and at times we were living on sips of water. Cordite from bursting shells causes your mouth to get drier and drier. I met Fred as often as possible and did my best to keep the communication lines open despite the shelling going on day and night.

It was now October 8th, and we learnt that 'A' Coy and part of 'B' Coy were going to attack the German part of Gun Trench that evening. Fred was there with Lieutenant Matthews, and I was at Headquarters ready to go in behind the attack to establish the wiring. Well, it appears that Gun Trench was one of the top defensive priorities of the German Defence system, so at the same time as we were preparing to attack, he was also massed to attack, intending to push us further back. Well neither our fellows nor Jerry were able to advance much. I heard later on that Tom Harris showed immense bravery and personally challenged the Germans to come out into the open and fight like men. Of course, they didn't and maintained their defensive positions. We suffered heavy losses, and the first officer of the Battalion was killed that night. His name was Lieutenant Heath of 7 Platoon, 'B' Coy. Fred was hit and badly shaken by a blow from a bursting shell splinter that connected with his shoulder. After treatment by the doctor, he went back to Lieutenant Matthews who was with 8 Platoon. The whole Battalion was now in desperate need of food and water.

The next morning, about 8 o'clock, Sergeant Dale told Jack Wilson, "Tug", and me to go and try and get a line through to the part of 'B' Coy who were cut off at the top end of Gun Trench. Tug was now working with me on the wiring. It appears that a small section of Gun Trench had been taken the previous night and two platoons, under Captain Towse were there. To get to them, we had to pass through a section of trench held by the Guards. We started from where the Headquarters were situated, which was a captured German dugout.

While we were going through the section occupied by the Guards, we met our Adjutant. He asked us where we were going and we told him that Sergeant Dale had ordered us to lay a line to 'B' Coy. He said to go back as he had just tried to reach them and the shelling had been too intense to get through. We asked his permission to give it a try, and he agreed. We did try, and we went part of the way with the aid of the Guardsmen. One of their officers saw us and ordered us to go back. He told us that his men were getting killed along the route that we needed to go. He said that the Germans were concentrating their fire on that section of Gun Trench. All that separated 'B' Coy from the Germans was a barrier made of sandbags. Well we obeyed the
Guards Officer and went back and found the Adjutant waiting for us. He quietly said, 'you couldn't get through could you.

'No Sir,' we both said.

'I admire you for trying,' he replied. He was a fine serving officer who we all had a lot of respect for.

Later that morning, when the German guns eased up from their heavy shelling, Tug and I started off again to install a line. We succeeded in getting through to our comrades this time and weren't they keen to see us. There were between thirty and forty of them under Captain Towse, and our two signallers there were unharmed. As soon we had the wires connected, the Captain got talking to the Adjutant at Headquarters. We interrupted him to let him know that we were heading back. He told us to stay there with him as he was short of men, and he expected the Germans to counterattack. So for the rest of the day and part of the night, we stayed there. The chaps had been through an appalling time sitting in an open trench with German shells falling all around them. Mercifully, only a few were killed. We had no option but to stay with the Captain and his men. I am sure that Captain Towse offered up a few prayers to God for us that day, as he was a good Christian man. It wasn't many weeks later before he himself was killed by a shell.

We were relieved that night by the East Surrey Regiment; they were one of our sister Battalions in the 37th Brigade. We went back to a reserve trench where we were served with food and water to drink. We hadn't had a wash and clean up for about ten days. Well, by October 13th, we were again laying wires to our 'A,' 'B' and 'C' Coys who were now in support of the Buffs. It appeared that this time it was the Buffs and the East Surreys who were to carry out an attack on Gun Trench. They took the trench those Surrey boys, but what havoc the Germans played with the Buffs. They lost the best part of three companies, including their Commanding Officer. Len Bush, who had just joined them, was lucky as he was with the last company and they were held back and not sacrificed as the other's had been. Our fellows had many casualties because the Germans were shelling all the trenches, including the reserve and support ones; they were extremely accurate and did massive damage. We took over from where the Buffs had been prior to the attack and the next day we were relieved by the Middlesex Regiment. We went off to what we hoped would be uninterrupted rest at Vermelles. The next day we were issued with some fresh clothes, and we were at last able to get a decent wash which meant some sort of a bath.

A couple of days later our Commanding Officer had us all on parade, and he read us a message from our Brigadier congratulating us for the fine job that we had done in the last few days. Len Bush told Fred and me that, they, the remnant of the Buffs, were put on parade and the General Officer Commanding the 1st Army, of which we were now part, came in person to thank and shake the hands of those of the Buffs who had survived. He was none other than General Sir Douglas Haig, and he it was who became Commander in Chief of the BEF a few days later when General French was relieved of his command. French had been responsible for the debacle which was now called The Battle of Loos.

The next task for the Royal West Kents was to go in support of one of the regiments of the 36th Brigade who were to attack the left part of the Hohenzollern Redoubt. This attack seemed to have been hastily put together, for, while we were passing through this part of the front line we saw, dug into the parapet facing the German lines, cylinders, which meant gas was going to be used. They were spaced thirty to forty feet apart. When we were brought in to support this attack, I guessed correctly what it was all about.

The attack opened with heavy artillery fire from our guns. We, the Royal West Kents, were in the open support trench ready to go to the help of those in the front line, which was about three hundred yards away. I was with the Battalion HQ staff, and suddenly the Adjutant climbed onto the parapet and scanned the area with his binoculars, so I, and I was the only one of our chaps who did it, got up and stood beside him. The gas attack was starting, and I saw the gas gradually rise from those cylinders, form a white cloud, and this cloud rose to about six to eight feet above the ground. All the separate gas clouds joined together and, with a west breeze behind the cloud went towards the German lines. Behind the gas cloud, walking in orderly fashion were the infantry. This time they were keeping behind the gas and not belting into it as the Scots had done. Those fellows took that trench on the October afternoon. The Adjutant was satisfied, and so was I for I think that we saw the last gas attack by either side in the war. I should think this happened about October 25th or 26th as I wrote in my diary that the 36th Brigade returned to the trenches and we supported them.

So ended the first terrible chapter of our immersion into war at its worst. I was told that Herb Ashdown, Ethel's cousin from Platt, had been wounded, but thankfully not too seriously. He was serving in 'A' Coy. Herb lasted until the summer of 1917 when he was killed. We stayed around the back of the trenches at various villages, resting. On October 21st we were inspected by the new Divisional General, General Scott, who told us how pleased he was at our behaviour in the recent attacks on the German trenches. I should say that our previous Divisional General, named Wing, was killed by a shell, along with his Adjutant, on the afternoon before the battle re-opened when he was having a close look at the proposed battlefield. General Scott was appointed immediately afterwards.

Well, both the Buffs and the West Kents were resting at a big village called Verquin, and we saw Len Bush who was now a Lance Corporal, and also Walter Springett, whose home adjoined the home of Ethel's parents at Bourne Farm, Plaxtol. Over the winter months, we kept bumping into these fellows as they had both been serving in the 2nd Buffs, were both wounded and sent home to recover. When they returned, they were placed in the 6th Buffs.

I must tell you what occurred on October 24th. Our mother's birthday would be on October $29^{th,}$ so I put five shillings, and Fred put eight shillings in a green envelope to send to her for her Birthday. I also enclosed two shillings for Ethel. We were told that it had got through at the base. Once earlier I had sent Ethel three or four shillings in a green envelope. It was opened by a base censor who changed it into a postal order and wrote Ethel a note telling her to warn her boyfriend not to send money like that again. Wasn't he honest? I always had a supply of English notes as we used to sell French Francs to new chaps so as they could buy things in France.

Towards the end of October, we had to return to those terrible trenches at the Hohenzollern Redoubt, which we had been in before. This was to be our depot for the next six or seven months. We were now part of the army holding this part of the line and up in front was the German stronghold of the Redoubt of which only a small amount had been captured despite massive losses. The weather had got worse, and there was now a lot of rain falling. As we were in the chalk district, the mud started to accumulate in the trenches. It was alright if you were in an old German dugout, for those had been dug deeply and were well built and ventilated. The front line had it bad as they were in between the captured German dugouts and the Germans themselves.

We continued to get letters from home and friends, and dear Ethel wrote regularly, and we received parcels too. It was our only contact with the real world where people lived normal lives. But the winter was fast approaching, and the weather was getting worse.

The Germans shelled continuously, and our gunners were running out of ammunition. One evening, after we had been heavily bombarded in the support line, Captain Towse begged the artillery officer over the telephone to retaliate. The artillery officer said that he was sorry, but, unless it was an S.O.S., he dared not fire any more shells that day. He explained to the Captain that he was restricted to only fire three shells per gun per day. Well about this time Officers started to go on leave. Privates had to wait six months, or more, officers only three months. Some officer on leave leaked the information about the shell shortage to the London Daily Mail, and it printed an article saying that it was a scandal that men were being killed in Flanders and there were no shells to return fire with. It appears that people were shocked and they didn't believe what Lord Northcliffe was telling them. It was said by people who knew that the Daily Mail was publicly burned on the floor of the London Stock Exchange for publishing such a lie. Well, it was accurate enough, and it was not long before Mr Lloyd George was appointed Munitions Minister. He it was who somehow got cracking and got the guns and ammunition required to get next year's big offensive going. More about that later.

On November 8th, 1915, the likeable and very competent Captain Towse was killed by a German shell. He was in the support trench just outside the dugout, where the signallers operated from. Well, the shell came directly onto him. He didn't stand a chance. Not only had we lost a good officer, but, having served in the South African war, he was much more tolerant and kind to us all. I'd like to say a few more words about him. His home was close to Bromley in Kent, and his dear wife always wrote to him on a daily basis, and she enclosed in her letter a cigarette. She knew, as he had told us, signallers, what a generous guy he was because he always gave his cigarette to others. She assumed that he at least was able to smoke at least one cigarette a day. It was a game he played just to please her.

Now it was the custom for the Commanding Officer of each company to send a verbal report over the telephone each night just before midnight. This report went to the Adjutant at Battalion HQ. A few weeks before Captain Towse was killed, he came, as usual, sat down beside the phone; however, instead of talking to the Adjutant, he took a box of matches out of his pocket, putting them on the table, which was usually an empty ammunition box. He just sat and waited. He did this on two consecutive nights, and, after talking to the Adjutant, he put the matches back in his pocket and wished us good night. It was then that Jack Webb had a brainwave and suggested that the Captain was probably trying to ask a question. I asked him what it was and he said that he must be looking for a fag.

Well, the Captain came the next night, took the box of matches from his pocket and placed them beside the telephone; Jack Webb then said; 'Would you like a cigarette, Sir?' The Captain nodded his head. The Captain told us that it was an offence for him to ask a ranker for a cigarette or any favour. The code of an officer forbids him ever to ask a favour, at any time, from us.

The Captain enjoyed smoking his cigarette before he spoke to the Adjutant and he gratefully accepted two or three more fags to take away and smoke. Each night after that, until his death, the signallers of 'B' Coy made sure that our officer never went to bed in the trenches without a last smoke. We were very saddened when he was killed.

Chapter 11

We were tragically losing friends and comrades on a regular basis. We were also receiving replacements to make up the numbers in the Coy. Some of these had been with us in the Battalion, had been wounded, recovered, and were now being added to our compliment. We were extremely fortunate to get them as they were some of the finest soldiers you could have in your Coy. I should have said that after the Loos attack Sergeant Dale rearranged his signallers. He gave me the chance to be on 'B' Coy's phone and to give up the linesman job. So I was able to see Fred often and he, in turn, used to keep me supplied with extra food. I have always believed that if it hadn't been for Fred's help with additional food that the officers didn't need, I should never have lasted that winter through. Such a lot of the fellows were falling sick and ending up in the hospital, and the food shortage seemed as bad as the shell shortage.

After the death of Captain Towse, 'B' Coy had no Commanding Officer. Captain Parker had already been promoted to Major and had left us to become Commanding Officer of the 8th Royal West Kents who had been so severely decimated when they were flung into the Loos offensive and who's Commanding Officer had been killed. The following Officers were the ones we still had in 'B' Coy: Lieutenant Harris of 6 Platoon and Lieutenant Matthews of 8 Platoon. Lieutenant Mann of 5 Platoon had been wounded and was still away recovering, and Lieutenant Heath of 7 Platoon had recently been killed. These latter two officers had been replaced by newcomers who had zero war experience.

So, for a while, 'B' Coy was commanded by one or other of the two senior Lieutenants, and that is how it was for the remainder of 1915.

As November arrived, so did the pouring rain and cold nights. We were all issued with the full rum ration at night and at stand-to in the morning. The tot had to be handed to you by an officer who was in charge of the rum jar, except on odd occasions which I will tell you about later.

The heavy shelling from the Germans continued as they were keen to get their captured trenches back. We occupied one of the captured German trenches and benefitted from their excellent deep warm dug-outs. As signallers, we had to have some form of shelter for our phone, so we were allotted a dug-out. 'B' Coy cooks and servants often shared it with us, and they always seemed to be able to prepare meals for their officers.

But what was the situation with the chaps? We, and this means the infantry, had all been issued with a greatcoat on enlistment and this was all right in normal conditions; however, the conditions weren't normal, and the fellows were often up to their waists in mud and water while in the trenches. The weather was getting very cold at nights and fellows had no alternative but to put their greatcoats on. Before long the lower half of the coat was just one mass of mud and water, as, of course, were their trousers and puttees. Some of the chaps in 'B' Coy in desperation cut off the lower half of their greatcoats making it into a three-quarter size. This alteration was fine while they were in the trenches, but when they went back to the rest area, they were singled out and put on a charge. The outcome as far as I can remember was that £2 was deducted from their pay to buy a new greatcoat. You can imagine that this action wasn't very popular amongst the chaps. They were issued with new greatcoats, and the other was taken away from them.

It was about this time that we were issued with a new type of jacket called a 'Jerkin'. This new coat had leather outside and was similar to the ones worn by Officers. It was noticeable that the officers didn't suffer like the rankers. The Jerkin was fleece lined inside, and there were no sleeves. A man's shoulders were covered, but their arms were free to be able to use their rifle. This new coat was a Godsend to us all and solved the problem with the greatcoat. When it was buttoned up over our tunics, it, not only kept your body warm but it was also waterproof. At last, someone had come up with something of use to us. In future, our greatcoats stayed in our backpacks, and our Jerkins were our best friend.

Duckboards were created for the floor of the trenches, making it a lot easier to walk where they were in place. With constant shelling occurring, the chalk sides gave way making the trench a big slimy pit. Rumour had it that we lost one fellow without trace. The fellows said that he drowned in the mud and water when he slipped off the duckboards. We were now doing about four days and nights in the line at a time, rather than the six we had been doing previously. The trenches that had been captured were still being heavily bombarded by the Germans. They obviously wanted them back so as they could recreate their fortress.

Ethel's Birthday would be on November 24^{th,} but I was unable to buy a card or send her anything. She would now be twenty-one as was Fred.

Towards the end of November, we went out of the line for a rest at the village of Annequin. We were able to stay in some new mineworkers cottages. These were being built when the war started and didn't have any roofs, windows or doors, but, other than that they were satisfactory. At the end of the road was a mine shaft and we used to put money in a kitty to buy some coal from the pithead. This area was one of the main mining regions of France. The main pits were at Lens which wasn't too far away but was in German hands.

Tom Harris from Halling and Bert Harris from Snodland had each been appointed a Lance Corporal, and Lieutenant Matthews was still on at me to leave the signals and accept an NCO's position in my old platoon, but I was very happy where I was. I regretted my decision later as you will find out.

During those awful weeks in November, Fred continued to keep us signallers supplied with extra food. The officers always seemed to have plenty to eat and drink; whiskey from England and extra Rum, but their life was also a bit more dangerous than ours. They wore the Sam Browne belt which the German snipers looked for when we were going over the top. If they killed the officers there was a fair chance that the attack would fail; that appeared to be the enemy's logic. Later in the war, the officers wore the same sort of tunic as we did and they left their Sam Browne belts behind. Even after the tunic change, the mortality rate of officers was always very high especially the junior officers who were expected to lead their men into battle when we went over the top.

Towards the end of November, when we were out of the line and resting, we went and watched our Battalion football team perform. Each regiment in our Brigade had a team made up of Officers, Non-Commissioned Officers and men. These chaps on our team were all quite good players. Back in our early days of training in England, we had the whole forward line from Northfleet Football Team, playing for us. At the time Northfleet were the Champions of Kent. Even at this stage of the war, we had a good team. Late in 1915 one match, I have recorded the result of was the Royal West Kent Regiment versus the East Surreys. We won 8 - 2. The games were played in good spirit as it was a light relief for everyone.

We all moved to a rest area in a large town beyond Bethune. The East Surreys and the West Kents were all billeted in the same building but on separate floors. It was a huge factory, and the floors that we slept on were used to dry tobacco leaves. There still was a considerable quantity of tobacco grown in Northern France, and we used to watch the old men and women cultivating the fields where the tobacco was normally grown. It was a hard task for the old people. They didn't use the factory while we were in that region of France.

About the second week of December, we were out of the trenches and were going on route marches in and around the district. We stayed at various villages, but not for more than one night at each village. Both Fred and I, plus many more, were feeling unwell and on one route march Fred fell out and later was given eights day confinement to barracks by the Medical Officer. I should say that after Ethel's Birthday, when we were staying in Bethune, I bought Ethel some coloured flowery handkerchiefs and I managed to post them to her. A bit late but she understood my situation. We were able to have regular baths in Bethune, and we were also issued clean clothing.

Another of my little stories now. One of our signallers, named Bill Norburn, had his home at Chipstead, near Sevenoaks. Bill had been promoted Corporal by Sergeant Dale and he it was who took over the wiring job from me. He was being helped by two signallers named Moffat, from Tottenham, and Mankelow from Tunbridge Wells. Now in Bethune, as in most French villages, the ladies used to try and eke out a living by turning one room in their houses into a kind of tea room, but, instead of serving tea they served us coffee. They fixed the price of a cup of coffee at around two cents, but we always enjoyed the coffee and also the heat of the room and the good chats that we had with our friends. These French ladies, God bless them, enjoyed our company too, for most of them had husbands away fighting in war.

Now in Bethune, in the High Street, a new lady started selling coffee from her house, and Bill and his pals were customers of hers. She asked, by sign language, one day, if someone would print her up a notice that she could put in her window advertising the fact that she sold coffee. Well Bill, who was always a bit of a wag, volunteered to create the notice. On a large piece of card he wrote in big letters – "TICKETS FOR BLIGHTY SOLD HERE" – Blighty was the Indian word for

England, but we also used it in France. Well her trade flourished, and the card hung in that window all the time that we were in that part of the line and used to go to Bethune to rest. Nobody ever told her what it meant, but she was happy and made a bit of a living, and that meant a lot to her.

A few days before Christmas we were suddenly told that we were moving up towards Festiubert and, on December 23rd, we relieved the East Surreys in the support line at Festiubert. This meant that we had to stay in the back line which was not even dug out yet. It was built up on top of the ground because of the amount of flooding. The East Surreys were taken out to have Christmas Day in billets. While the chaps of 'B' Coy were waiting to take over, a single German shell fell amongst them, fired from about a quarter of a mile away. A fragment of this shell killed Company Sergeant Major Smith instantly. Fortunately, nobody else was hit. Talk about a bullet or shell having your name on it! CSM Smith was a fine soldier, a regular soldier from the 1st Battalion who had been wounded on the retreat from Mons. After a recovery period in England, he had rejoined us as Company Sergeant Major in 'B' Coy. He was well liked by the chaps as were all the old timers who came to us from the regular battalions which existed before the war. Their discipline was perfection, and nothing fazed them.

On Christmas Eve, 2015, our rations consisted of biscuits and bully, and it poured with rain. Although we signallers had a dugout, everything was wet and miserable. On Christmas Day we were able to fry some bacon and had the same for dinner plus some pieces of bread. In addition, we were able to have a piece of Christmas pudding which made a nice change. Now in front of where we were, was the proper British front line, but it was standing half full of water. The La Bassee canal wasn't far off, and we wondered whether the Germans were pumping the water out of their trenches and it was flowing into ours. There was one platoon which had been sent to man the outpost in this front line trench and with this platoon was an officer. Each platoon spent just twenty-four hours in this dreadful trench, but two stretcher bearers and two signallers were told to spend forty-eight hours there because of the shortage of key men. The first spell of duty was by Harry Durden and Jack Webb, and on Christmas night it was Harry Munday's and my turn. Harry was a bugler but had joined us to make up the number of signallers required. As it got dark, we moved off over the top to the front line. All went well until we had to cross a stream using a plank. We were wearing waders which came up to our thighs. I slipped and fell into the creek and sank up to my neck. The water flowed down my neck, inside my clothes and into my waders. They eventually managed to pull me out, but I was wet through. We took over the phone which meant sitting on ammunition boxes with water up to our waist, and we had to make sure that the phone was well clear of the water. Lieutenant Matthews was in charge of the party that I went up with. He gave me a good tot of rum, which, because I was wet through, sent me to sleep for about twelve hours. When I awoke, it was midday Boxing Day. When I asked him for my share of the rum, which he was then dispensing to the others, he suggested that I would be better off not having any. Harry Munday said that he couldn't believe how I had just slept. Well, that night Lieutenant Matthews and his party left, and another group arrived under the command of a new officer.

Someone nicked the rum, and the new officer didn't feel strong enough to tackle the men and see where it had gone. We had no rum ration for the next twenty-four hours. It wasn't until Harry, and this officer and I were leaving the trench; the rest of the party had gone, and the chaps of the Essex hadn't arrived to take over. We noticed, lying face up in the water, one of the group who had come up twenty-four hours ago. We propped him up beside the trench. He was out cold, and we quite correctly assumed that he was the one who had stolen the jar of rum. He had drunk himself insensible.

The officer told us that we would have to carry him back to the main trench. I told him that we wouldn't do it and I sent Harry to connect up the phone again and ring Sergeant Dale. The Sergeant, together with the Adjutant, hadn't left the command post as he wasn't sure that we had all got out. The Adjutant said to prop him up in the trench, and he would get chaps with the Essex Regiment sent with a stretcher to bring this drunk back. It ended up taking four stretcher bearers most of the night to get him back; all because he became too greedy and drank himself almost to death. We heard later that it was touch and go whether he would ever regain consciousness, but he eventually came around. He was put on a charge, but I never heard what the outcome was.

Chapter 12

We left the trenches at Festiubert and were not sorry because the conditions were terrible. We moved back behind the lines to have New Year at rest. Our small group of signallers enjoyed themselves at Headquarters as Sergeant Dale, fine organiser that he was, had been able to get a nice meal and party for us. Our French friends also enjoyed themselves. I would like to say that the whole time that I was in France and Belgium, we were always treated very kindly by the inhabitants who were also living under very difficult circumstances.

Our next stay in the line was not far away at a place called Givenchy. It being winter and just into the year of 1916; we felt the severe cold. Many chaps had fallen sick during the last few months and returned to base or to hospital. As a result of all the drop outs we were getting new faces amongst us on a continual basis; some old soldiers and some new ones. We did quite a lot of work as reserves for regiments which were in the line from Festiubert downwards. The German artillery was superior to ours as they fired considerably more rounds than ours did. We went, on a few occasions, to the Tobacco Factory at Bethune, and I remember that we went to a cinema, the only time I went while we were in Flanders. There was also a divisional boxing tournament held at Bethune which we were able to attend. I remember that the West Kents had the heavyweight champion. Our man beat a clever boxer from the Queens. This boxer of ours had been heavyweight champion of the Navy in peacetime. He had finished his service and left the Navy. When war broke out he had signed up with the infantry as he said that he wanted a change. He had a job with our transport section. I have never seen anybody hit so hard. He just stood flat footed and walloped his opponents. Our regimental football team got through to the final of the Divisional Shield, beating the Norfolk Regiment 6 – 0. Sorry, that was the semi-final, they, in fact, were beaten 1 – 0 by the Royal Fusiliers in the final.

I was feeling very unwell during the early weeks of 1916, and many other chaps were also feeling the strain. We should have been withdrawn from trench duty and taken back for a rest; however, the Generals in charge always liked to have plenty of reserves waiting around in the mud and water, and my word we had been in some mud. We were still being kept out of front line duty as February came along. We were still moving from place to place as reserves, just behind the lines. The weather was freezing, but we were usually able to find a billet to sleep in.

We had now all been issued with a much-improved gas mask which we called a smoke helmet. This helmet went right over our head with eyepieces to see through. This device was the gas mask that I had to wear for the rest of my time serving in France. On February 10th we, the Royal West Kents, were inspected by General Scott, our divisional commander. He presented the prizes won by our chaps at the various sports which had been held recently.

On February 19th, something happened that was new to us. Up to this point, we had only seen the odd German plane in the sky, and, also, our side only had a few biplanes. This specific day; however, a number of German aircraft dropped bombs on Bethune and the surrounding area. We observed three bombs explode in Bethune and the next day we saw about twenty German planes in the sky flying in formation. So things had changed, and the war had taken to the air as well. Up to now, there had only been the occasional dog fight between one plane from each side and no bombing.

On February 20th, we were told that we were returning to our old position in the line at Vermelles. This explained why we had been given a fair few weeks out of the front line. We, evidently, were now going to be involved in an offensive. By February 22nd we were back on trench duty. Snow fell for the first time that winter and Captain Matthews, who had been on leave, was back on duty. He was duly appointed Officer Commanding 'D' Coy, and he, together with Fred, left 'B' Coy to take up his new appointment. Now we also had to have a new Commanding Officer as our Colonel, who was pretty old, had left us to be replaced by a much younger officer from the Royal Welsh Fusiliers. His name was Lieutenant Colonel Owen. He wore his old cap badge and also his ribbons at the back of his cap. Major Beeching, our second in command, had also left together with all the other Company Commanders. It seems as if they had done their job in bringing us to the correct level of soldiering proficiency and now younger, less experienced, officers could lead us. 'B' Coy had Lieutenant Harris appointed as their captain and Officer Commanding and Captain Dawson of 'C' Coy, took over command of the company.

I would now like to mention a bit about ourselves. All of us were volunteers, and no-one much regretted joining the Army when we did in August 1914 or even joining later as the war progressed. Everyone believed that it was the Germans or us. We were being promised, back in England, by people who knew better than we did, a land fit for heroes to live in when the war finally finished. In the pre-war years, how difficult it had been to get a living but that would be all in the past for those who had served. Of course, only those who survived would be able to remember the promises. There was very little disobedience amongst the chaps, and it was only the odd man or two who got into trouble. When we were out of the line resting or sitting in a respectable dug-out in the trenches, the main topic discussed soon became – 'How long is this bloody war going to last?' To our eyes, neither side looked as if they were capable of winning, so the answer was usually – 'It will end when enough of us poor blighters have been killed, and they run out of soldiers.' Even in those days, people were under the delusion that there were too many people in the world, so, some said; it was a way of reducing the world population. That theory was alright provided it wasn't you who was included in the reduction.

On February 25th, we were back at the old battlefields, and we were back in billets at Annequin, which was in the support trenches. An Irish Brigade was holding our front line which we had been in the previous November, and they were new to warfare. The Germans were now experts in the use of their mortars and were able to judge the distance so accurately that they dropped a large proportion of their shells straight into our trenches. The land was also covered in snow.

Early on the morning of February 27th, we were assembled and went to take over from where the Irish regiment had been. They had withdrawn from the line leaving nobody holding that section. Now let me tell you a bit about the names given to trenches etc. This trench where we went back to was named Northampton Trench in honour of that regiment. There was also a trench named Gordon Trench in honour of the Gordon Highlanders. This part of the line was composed of chalk and all the winter of 1915 and 1916 our miners, who in peacetime mined coal, were tunnelling from our lines under the German lines. The Germans were doing the same thing. One day, when things were relatively quiet, we signallers, sitting by our phone, could detect the noise of a pick being used underneath us. We called Captain Harris, and he jovially said that he hoped that it was one of our chaps and not a German. This area was also known as the quarries because of all the mining. As I have said previously, the Germans had constructed a fortress here, and it required some taking. It was called the Hohenzollern Redoubt and had been built like a fortress. At present we had only taken a few trenches in the outer part of it, but each day we kept trying to take more, and every day a small mine would go off under the German lines.

We stayed a couple of days or so in the line and then went back for a few days to Bethune in the tobacco factory. We were on stand-to duty, which meant that we could be sent back to the trenches at an hour's notice. We sensed that something was afoot. It was now March 5th, and in the last few hours, I should say, our miners had blown the biggest set of mines so far on the Western Front and mostly right under the German front line which had disappeared. I felt sorry for the poor chaps who had been in those trenches even if they were the enemy.

The largest section, which was parallel to Northampton Trench, must have been fifty to sixty yards across and earth and Germans had just vanished. On March 6th the Buffs attacked and were able to hold these craters. There was one enormous one and then four or five smaller ones. These craters were situated on the high ground stretching along where the German front line had been. We, the Kents, were sent up to support the Buffs and suffered many casualties, mostly from the heavy bombardment from the German guns who were shelling their old positions. In anticipation of the attack, they had the exact location of their former trenches recorded for their artillery, so their guns were more accurate than usual.

We were now involved in a battle with a vengeance. The mud in the trenches and in the bottom of the craters was deep, and it was still snowing. I didn't see Fred for several days and all in all it was a very tough time. We relieved the Buffs, who had gone through a terrible time defending the craters and had lost a large number of men. They were exhausted after the massive German counterattack to retake their trenches, or craters as they now were. Here it was, with us in close support, that Corporal Cotter of the Buffs earned his Victoria Cross. Although he was severely wounded, he urged his pals not to give in, and everyone knew that it was this gallant Buff NCO who saved that part of the line from being retaken by the Germans. He later died from his wounds at Vermelles.

Now it was the West Kent's turn to hold these mine destroyed German trenches. One Coy was occupying it at a time, or should I say one company plus its bombers. Each Company now had a section of expert Mills bomb throwers attached to it. The men of this section were able to throw the bombs like cricket balls very accurately and could hit the German saps, which were projections from the German front line. They caused a lot of damage to men and material; however, unfortunately, we ran out of the hand grenades when we needed them most.

Our 'D' Coy, under the command of Captain Matthews, was the first company to hold the craters. The Germans tried to bomb and shell them out, but they survived. On March 9th it was 'B' Coy's turn to go up and hold them. Sergeant Dale withdrew Harry Durden from the signallers. He put me in charge with Jack Webb and a chap who had just arrived from England. We went in to take over just before it got dark. I hadn't seen Fred for a few days now and was getting a bit worried for his safety.

A fire-step had been dug into the lip of the biggest crater, and this is where we signallers were placed. A hole had been made to allow the phone plus one signaller to take shelter. Over this, a piece of galvanised iron had been put to keep both the phone and signaller dry. This crater was a pretty hot spot, so I put Jack Webb manning the phone. He was in direct contact with the artillery officer behind and he, in turn, had a number of howitzer guns ready for immediate action.

The only phone lines that we had on our set were artillery lines, and there were none to our Headquarters.

As so often happened, the artillery would not send an officer or man to work their phone when the job was as dangerous as it now was. The new chap got up on the fire step to use his rifle if that was needed. I took my bayonet off my rifle and told Webb that, if necessary, I would fight a hand to hand fight while he would let the artillery officer know what was happening. It was a very tense situation, and we all felt very vulnerable. So we waited, everybody alert, but, where was Captain Harris? He should have been with me by now so as he could give the order for the guns to fire if we were attacked. We waited, still no officer, and then the chaps on the fire step said; 'The bastards are coming, the whole bloody trench over there is packed with Germans.'

Well, the Germans got out of their trench, which was about one hundred yards away and started coming towards us. It was still too far for our bomb throwers, and there were masses of Germans approaching. Where was Captain Harris? Webb kept saying: 'the shells are in the heavy guns, the gunners are ready to let loose and we don't have an Officer to give the order to fire.' When the Germans were about thirty yards away from me, I wasn't waiting any longer and gave the order to fire. The gunners of ours knew how to use their guns, and the response was instant. The Germans out in the open were decimated and the others, still coming out of their trench, decided to abandon the attack.

The Gunners reloaded and continued to rake the German trench with shrapnel for that is what they were firing. A lot of the enemy were killed that day right in front of our eyes. As the attack petered out and ceased, along came Captain Harris. It appeared that he had initially gone to the end crater to check that everything was alright there and this was quite a distance from where we were with the telephone. When the Germans emerged from their trenches, he had tried to get to me. With the Germans attacking he had to take a detour by returning to our lines and then coming from there to the crater. He congratulated me for making the decision to tell the artillery to fire. The mud was knee deep, and it was pretty cold.

'Get on to the guns,' the Captain shouted. 'Tell the artillery officer to keep sending shells onto their lines to give them something to think about.'

The fact that I had given the order was against regulations. Us Signallers had been told never to give an order down the phone unless it had been given by an officer. I should have been in terrible trouble but, instead, had been complimented by my officer. Well as soon as those chaps of ours, who hadn't been killed or injured by the German shelling, saw what had happened, they started to sing the West Kent marching song which had been handed down to us by the regulars. As it was a quiet frosty night, that song was heard by the Buffs who were in support of us about half-a-mile behind where we were. Len Bush told me about hearing us sing when I next met him. He said that it was very moving.

Well, we were relieved the next day by the Buffs. The mud was still knee deep in Gordon Alley which led out of the crater area, and we just changed places with the Buffs in the Reserve trench. There were a few dugouts here which gave us some cover from the elements and was greatly appreciated by us. Well, the German sappers had not been idle for they had mined under where the craters were. While the Buffs were holding this area, they blew some of the mines, killing many of the Buffs. I hadn't seen my brother for a week now, and it was also impossible to shave or wash. Water shortage was acute because the Germans were continually shelling our transport and rear positions. We just had to carry on. Fortunately, I never had to go into those craters again. We always seemed to be in reserve to another regiment which suited me just fine.

Reflections - Chapters 9 to 12

In the last four chapters, nine to twelve, it is evident from what Sid tells us that the war is intensifying and the day to day casualties are increasing. More of Sid's friends and others he knew who came from the region where he lived in Kent have been killed.

His account of what happened at the Battle of Loos is difficult to fathom, and, if he hadn't seen what happened at first hand, it would be hard to believe that it actually took place.

The Royal West Kent Regiment were included in the battle plan for the Loos Offensive. One would have thought that all the experienced troops required for the first major British offensive of the war should have been in place before the attack was launched. As he describes in his account, when they should have been at Loos, they were, in fact, sitting by the side of the road in the Armentières sector waiting for the Canadians to arrive. They could not leave the area and move to the Loos Battlefield until they were relieved.

Unbelievably, when the attack started, their replacements, the Canadians, were still in Folkestone. They hadn't even landed France. In fact, it was a further two days before they reached where the West Kents were located.

To compound the stupidity of the situation, when the 6th Battalion, Sid's Battalion, didn't arrive, they threw the 8th Battalion of the Royal West Kents, who had freshly arrived in France, into the fight in place of them. None of that draft, other than a few of the NCO's and Officers, had been anywhere near action before. It wasn't a great surprise when a large number of them were killed on their first day at the front. One of those killed was the Commanding Officer.

As Sid said in his account, surely they could have planned the whole event better and saved a lot of the lives that were lost. The fact General French was removed as the Commander of the BEF after this debacle, points the finger of blame at him, but it doesn't bring back any of those brave men who lost their lives at Loos.

As I have said before, it is very easy to be critical one hundred years after the event, but if even a Private could see what had happened was inept and how easily it could have been corrected, then criticism of those in charge is justified. The Generals' solution to the problem of the non-appearance of the Canadian Army, was to throw inexperienced soldiers into the line. The result was carnage on a grand scale as most of the rest of the offensive had also been poorly planned. In fairness to the Generals, they were forced to proceed on the scheduled date because of a promise to the French.

About a year ago I stood on a spot in the little village called Hulluch on the Loos battlefield. The exact place I was standing on is where the German machine gunners were set up to enfilade the British troops as they attacked across the countryside directly in front of them. The British battalions had been ordered to attack the German trenches at Bois Hugo and Chalet Wood, which were to my left on higher ground. They were given the order to attack despite the knowledge that there were many well-entrenched machine guns positioned so as they could wipe them out. There was zero cover for the advancing troops. The cemeteries that I visited in the area, and that I could see from my vantage point in Hulluch, are a testimony to the disastrous mishandling of that attack. This locality is now the resting place of a vast number of those brave men who were mown down in their thousands. Unusually, three Generals lost their lives during the Battle of Loos, so shells are not selective in whom they kill as they were all behind the frontline.

We are introduced to the horrors of gas in this section of the book. Sid's personal observations of the plight of the Gordon Highlanders, who had attacked in the midst of the gas rather than behind it, is a horrific tale. The Generals knew that gas was going to be used as a weapon by either the Germans or themselves, but they hadn't done sufficient work in ensuring that their troops had a gas mask that could be used during an offensive operation. They supplied the men with an apparatus which, when worn, limited their breathing. This limitation meant that they couldn't wear the gas mask when they were on the move. It all seems a bit daft.

Sid also describes the problem that the shortage of shells caused near the end of 1915. Imagine only being able to fire three shells a day per gun when the Germans are shelling you without a break. Not good for the morale of the troops in the front line. The artillery officer had to explain that unless it was an S.O.S, he couldn't answer a demand for shelling. An S.O.S situation was when a section of trench was currently under attack, and they fired a 'very light' calling for shellfire to help them out. He had to reserve his allocation of shells in case he was asked to fire as a result of an S.O.S.

What the troops involved in the offensives found hard to understand was why they were being sacrificed in useless attacks when the planning hadn't been done. If they were trying to hold ground that had been taken, at great cost in men killed and wounded, they might then be told that there were no shells to help keep the Germans at bay. The front line troops had every right to get upset. They had no alternative but to follow orders and hold onto the ground their colleagues had won and died for even if there was no supporting gunfire. It naturally increased the number of defenders killed.

When I read about the lack of planning and the trouble that it caused, I naturally assumed that planning wasn't possible due to the large number of variables and the fact that it all had to be done on pieces of paper. I then learnt that one of the most successful Generals of the First World War was an Australian named Monash. He is also rated as being the most famous commander in Australian history.

A professional engineer, he was a Territorial Army officer before the war and ran his own very successful Construction Company. On the outbreak of war, he was appointed as the commander of the Australian 4th Infantry Brigade. He trained them and then sailed for Egypt and the Gallipoli campaign. With his engineering and construction background, he was meticulous in his planning. He was also strong enough to resist the pressures from his superiors when asked to proceed with an attack despite all the pieces of his jigsaw not being in place.

It was the same when he got to France. By then he was the Commander of the entire Australian contingent. If his troops were involved in an attack, then he would make sure that the plan was watertight. He also would not allow the timing to be altered if his troops were not ready. Most of what he was involved in was successful showing that planning was possible.

On many occasions, his superiors tried to bully him into attacking earlier than he had planned. At other times on the day agreed for an offensive, he hadn't been able to get everything lined up as per the plan. He would delay rather than launch the attack before his troops were totally ready. Of interest was the fact that his superiors never ordered the offensive to commence if he said he was not ready. That doesn't mean that he was happy to do everything that his superiors asked him to do. Field Marshal Haig tried to get rid of him on a number of occasions as he wouldn't 'jump' when ordered to do so. The Australian Prime Minister insisted that he remain as Commander of the Australian Army in France.

To run his construction company in Melbourne, Monash had to plan and consider all the options if he was going to be successful. He knew how to get results and also that the offensive would fail unless every aspect had been meticulously planned. Most of the other Generals were professional soldiers and had never been involved in running a successful operation. Planning to them was a straight jacket that they didn't want to wear; it also took a lot of time and resources which they needed to do other things. Don't get me wrong; they would do a certain amount of planning; however, if the ingredients of the plan weren't all in place when the attack was due to commence, they just went ahead and hoped for the best. The net result of 'hoping for the best', was the savaging of the 'Lions'. The example of the Canadians being still in Folkestone when the Battle of Loos commenced is a case in point. The 8th Battalion of the Royal West Kents was nearly wiped out because they were thrown into the offensive instead of experienced, battle-hardened, troops.

One of the factors starting to affect the effectiveness of the British Army was the lack of officers. The junior officers, who had come out to France in 1915, had mostly been killed or promoted. There was now a severe shortage at the lower level. It wasn't too bad in the battalions which had been in Flanders for some time as the regular troops were able to run the show and cover for the lack of officer expertise; however, in the new Battalions, there was a problem as the officers and their men were all inexperienced. This issue got worse as more and more of the experienced NCO's were killed. In addition to a lack of officers, most of the new drafts were made up of conscripts who didn't want to be at the front in the first place.

From remarks made by Sid, you can see that the members of the BEF still believed that they were fighting for a better life. One of the recruiting slogans was that the young men of England should go away and fight and by beating Germany, they would obtain a better life back home when the war was over. The hardships and difficulties that everybody in England faced before the war would be a thing of the past. There would be good jobs for everyone. After a while, in the trenches, this started to wear a bit thin, and there was the realisation that most of those fighting, wouldn't actually get home to enjoy the promise of a good life. They would have a permanent resting place in Flanders.

The story that Sid tells about the greatcoat brings out two opposing views. The men in the trenches had to cut the greatcoat because they were getting soaking wet and caked in mud which was weighing them down. Rather naturally, they cut off the bottom of the coat as they could hardly move around. Behind the lines, they met a 'Jobs Worth' Officer who put the men who had damaged Army property, on a charge. The end result of all this was that they had to buy a new greatcoat and throw away the modified one. They were also charged £2 each which was quite a sum in those days. The positive to come out of this story is that the powers that be had already realised that there was a problem and they issued a new leather coat called a Jerkin to all the troops. This was a leather coat which was tailor-made for their use in the trenches and became every Tommy's friend.

One of the factors that affected the morale of the frontline troops the most was the fact that the Germans fired a lot more shells than the allied artillery did. Certainly, that was the case at this stage of the war as there was still a shortage of shells. It was criminal to send troops into battle and not have the necessary ordinance to protect them or at least give the enemy as much back as they are giving you. The decision to move Lloyd George into the role of Munitions Minister seems to have sorted this particular problem out; however, the problem should have been sorted a lot earlier.

At the start of his account of the war in France, Sid describes the war as being gentlemanly. The picture he now paints is of being involved in a fierce encounter where you are very fortunate if you survive. What Company you are in makes a huge difference; if you are one of the first sent over the top in an attack, you probably won't survive. If you are the last over the top, then you may be ordered back if there is a high loss rate and you will survive. Very much luck of the draw.

One of the most dramatic battles that Sid was involved in took place in the craters at the Hohenzollern Redoubt close to Vermelles. It was here that Sid had to give the order to fire when the officer who was supposed to be with him hadn't arrived. He should have received a decoration for taking that decision but of course, there was no officer present, and in fact, the Captain wouldn't have recommended him because he was the one who was meant to be there. He wouldn't want to advertise the fact that he wasn't there at a critical time in the defence of the area.

The Hohenzollern Redoubt was a very strong German defensive position on the Loos battlefield. Sid was involved in the attacks on the redoubt during the month of March in 1916. The redoubt was north of Loos-en-Gohelle, a mining town north-west of Lens in France. The redoubt had been fought over since the Battle of Loos which had commenced in August 1915.

During the March attack by the British, the German garrison in the Hohenzollern Redoubt was doubled, and a high level of alert maintained until the end of the March. The Germans felt that the possibility of another British attack was unlikely as they entered the month of April. The 37th Brigade commander, Brigadier-General Cator, reported that the interiors of craters were man traps. The craters attracted artillery and mortar fire from the Germans but gave no protection to the British defenders, being confined spaces with a morass of liquid chalk and black mud at the bottom, which was unusable as a material for fortification. Building up crater lips with a parados (the embanked rear lip of the trench) or hurdles and boards failed because shell-fire soon dislodged them and the inner sides collapsed into the crater. Defending the forward lip had proved difficult, due to its breadth and the presence of clay mounds twelve to twenty feet high. These obstructed the field of fire. Cator recommended that the rear lips of craters or a line beyond them were better positions to occupy and the interiors of craters should be left empty, with positions maintained on the rear lips. Because of the incessant shellfire, other commanders suggested that the craters should be vacated as soon as possible to save more unnecessary slaughter.

Sid was very lucky to survive this particular area of the conflict.

Chapter 13

After about a week, during which time I hadn't met my brother, we were taken back behind Vermelles for a break. Thankfully, at last, I met Fred.

'They have been talking about you Sid, what have you been up to?' Was the first question that he fired at me.

'I haven't been up to anything special. What are you talking about,' I replied.

'You want to hear what my Governor is saying about you. He says that you are the tops; or something like that.'

It seemed to me that although Captain Harris wasn't big enough to mention Jack Webb or me in despatches that night to the Commanding Officer, he had been talking to the other officers about what we had done in the crater. Neither Webb nor I spoke to anybody about what happened in the crater when we had to give the order to the Artillery Officer to open fire. We also hadn't talked about it on the telephone. Because we had disobeyed orders and had given the order to fire despite an officer not being present, we could have been in real trouble. That's why we were keeping quiet about it. If we hadn't said anything, then Captain Harris was the only one who could have mentioned it, which was encouraging. Perhaps we weren't in trouble after all.

Life to us now was being in the reserve in trenches such as Kaiserin Trench, Lancashire Trench, Vigo Street, and so on. About the third week of March, we were taken back to rest at our old friend the Tobacco Factory. This building gave us room to have a decent sleep, and we also were able to tidy ourselves up a bit.

The Buffs also came out of the line and Fred, and I met Len Bush on a number of occasions. Now, after six months' service overseas in Flanders, it became possible for men and NCOs to be drawn for leave which would be for six days. Any person, whose name was chosen, was allowed to go home for a break. The officers, who were not killed or injured, usually had a leave-break after three months. Many chaps had been killed, wounded or fallen sick, so the numbers of those who had gone overseas in June 1915 had been severely depleted.

Each platoon in 'B' Coy used to put the names of all those who had not been on leave and who were eligible, into a hat and then someone drew the names. It was usual to send the two first names that came out of the hat on leave. Fred had just left 8 Platoon as Captain Matthews had been promoted and moved. In error, his name was put into 8 Platoon's hat with the others, although he was now in 'D' Coy. On March 22nd Fred's name was drawn for leave from 8 Platoon's hat, but it was immediately rejected by those conducting the draw. The committee in charge of the process was made up of corporals and privates. So poor Fred wasn't allowed to go home yet. When Captain Matthews heard of this from someone, it wasn't Fred or me; he arranged for Fred to go on leave on March 29th with the next batch from 'C' Coy. He departed about midday, saying cheerio to me and my pals with a big grin on his face. Lucky blighter.

I continued to get letters and parcels from dear Ethel and our parents and friends. One thing that we all prized was the regular delivery of the Kent Messenger. When we,

Fred and I, had finished reading it, we used to pass it around to others who were interested in the news and what was going on at home in Kent.

We continued to go into the trenches often in reserve or support to our own and other regiments. When we were out, we used to go to Bethune or to Annequin to recuperate. I was beginning to feel the strain of constant combat and at times felt very unwell. I didn't go to the doctor as I felt that the better weather would soon be upon us and my condition would improve.

Well, on April 2nd the draw for leave came around again. This time the 8 Platoon chaps sent for Bert Robinson, a signaller in 8 Platoon, to do the draw. By a stroke of luck, Robbo drew out my name, and not only my name, but Tug Wilson's name as well. This occurrence caused a bit of a row as two signallers names had been drawn by another signaller from 8 Platoon. Robbo told me later that, at first, the chaps wanted to throw back Tug and my names into the hat because we were based in Battalion HQ. Then they said to only throw mine out as they had done with my brother's a few days' earlier.

Robbo was the biggest fellow that we had in 8 Platoon; he told them if they did that then he would go and tell the Adjutant about it. The end of the argument was that Tug Wilson and I were selected to go on leave. Thank God that Robbo was doing the draw and that he stood up for me.

The battle in our sector was still going on with small mines going up almost every day, being detonated by the Germans and us. But on April 6th, the day after my birthday, I left the trenches on my leave break and marched with twenty-nine others from the battalion to a place called Noyelles, where our transport was based. The night before I was due to go on leave, Quarter Master Sergeant Kerslake brought me 100 Francs with my rations. I had to sign for them. When I told him that I hadn't that much to my credit, he just told me to sign for it and if you are in debt in the Army, you won't get killed. When I eventually changed it into English pounds, it was around £3.

At the transport hub, we were given a meal but no rations to take with us for the journey. It was a Thursday as far as I can remember. We had a wash but weren't given a clean shirt or other clothes. We were also pretty 'lousy'. I turned my puttees inside out so as they looked clean, but the caked mud was now against my legs. By evening we were ready for inspection by Captain Alderman, the Transport Officer. Corporal Tom Aspinall of 'C' Coy, who was a signaller, was also going on leave and he it was who was in charge of our party of thirty. After being inspected by Captain Alderman, he then said; 'I have one more thing to ask you before you leave and before you speak I want you to think long and hard about your answer. Have any of you got letters or messages that you are carrying home for someone else? If you have, please give them up, and they will be burned without anybody knowing who sent them or who they are going to. Well, I was now up against it good and proper. A friend of mine, when he heard that I was going on leave, asked me to post a letter to his wife. I hesitated a bit before taking it from him and asked him if it had anything to do with the war. 'No,' he said, 'it concerns my wife and me. My marriage is about to break up, and it's all about that.'

'I'll do it for you as long as that is the reason,' I said.

He added that it was too personal to send from France by post as he didn't want the censors reading his personal matters. Well, he was my friend, so I took a chance and folded the letter up, putting it inside my gas helmet. When Captain Alderman asked us the question, I remained quiet.

Well, we entrained at Bethune but not before a huge traction engine had run into us in the darkness. It smashed down one of the chaps who was going on leave, killing him instantly. It could so easily have been me, because, this chap, like me, was walking on the outside of the group and the wheel hit my shoulder bruising it quite badly. This traction engine was moving the only 15-inch gun on the Western Front on our side of the line. It had no lights, and neither did we. When we reached Bethune Station, Tom Aspinall reported what had happened, and the officer in charge at the station said that they would go back and recover this poor chap's body. After we had got back from leave, an inquiry was held, but no one was blamed. But how near it was for me; and I was carrying an illegal letter.

We left Bethune by train early the next morning and arrived at Boulogne about mid-morning. There were several hundreds of us from all different regiments heading towards the quays. Out of the blue, a chap walking beside me was stopped by an official looking man who asked him to accompany him somewhere to be checked. They were picking up people, possibly deserters, for checking at the port. After that initial alarm, everything went smoothly, and we travelled across the Channel to Folkestone where we entrained for

Victoria Station. The train we were on passed through Wrotham station, the station closest to my home, at high speed. At Victoria, I went to the kiosk to change my 100 Francs into pounds and from there saw the train I was hoping to catch departing without me. I dumped my kit onto one of the benches in the station and waited for two and a half hours for the next train to leave. There were very few passengers so I was able to dump my gear on one side of the carriage and I sat on the other side. I had great difficulty in trying to stay awake as I had been up most of the previous night. I kept awake until Swanley and the next thing I knew the guard was waking me up at Maidstone East Station, I had missed Wrotham station. I went up the hill to the Barracks where there was an old soldier on guard at the gates.

'Want a night's doss mate?' he asked me.

'Yes please, I am dead-beat,' I replied.

He let me through, and I went into the guard hut where I was given a mug of tea. The tea was the first warm drink that I had been given since Thursday morning.

'What time do you want to leave at in the morning?' the old soldier asked me.

'I want to get the first train that goes from Maidstone East to Wrotham,' I replied.

I was duly woken in time to have a cup of tea then walk down the hill to the station where I got a train arriving at Wrotham somewhere about 8 to 8.30am.

The first thing that I had to do was go to the Post Office where Mrs and Miss Callow greeted me. I bought a 1d stamp to put on my friend's letter and posted it. When I returned to join the Platoon in France, my friend thanked me for posting the letter. His wife had answered it, and a couple of weeks later he was given special leave to return home and sort out his marriage. When he came back from seeing her he told me that everything was now all right; so my good deed had paid off.

I walked the three and a half miles to my parents' home and surprised them by turning up so soon after Fred had been home. The first thing that I said to my mother was to light up the copper and get me some hot water. There were no bathrooms in those days. I said that I needed the biggest bath to be put in the scullery so as I could get all the muck off me from the outside. Meanwhile, some young people called Wisbey, who lived nearby, called to see if my mother required any shopping. I persuaded them to take a note to Basted Paper Mills for Ethel. All they needed to do was hand in the note at the office telling them that it was for Miss Ashdown, Ethel to me, and it was very urgent. When Ethel received the note, she said to the Foreman: 'I'm off, Sid's home and I won't be in for a few days.' In fact, she didn't work for the whole of the next week.

I had my bath. I threw my lousy grey black shirt out into the garden, together with my socks, trousers and tunic and I never wore them again until I was ready to return to France on the following Thursday evening. When we went on leave, we didn't get any rations or ration money. It wasn't much of a 'thank you' that when fellows went on leave for a week or more no ration money was given to them. They had to live off their wives or family. I had not eaten since Thursday morning, and it was now Saturday morning. One of the things about being at the front was that I had got used to being hungry. To me, the week at home was a rest that I badly needed. I visited Ethel's parents with her, and we also visited those at Oxon Hoath where I had worked before the war. I was asked a very surprising question there. Sir William Geary had a middle-aged lady working as his Secretary. Her father had previously been employed as the Steward to the estate.

'Now Sidney,' she said. 'Will you please answer me one question – How many Germans have you killed?'

'Miss Alcock,' I told her, absolutely horrified by her question; 'I have had quite enough to do making sure that the Germans don't kill me without going around counting dead Germans that I might have killed.'

That is all I told anybody about the war. Unfortunately, Fred had been home just before me, and he had told them a lot more than was good for them. He had told them stuff that they would have been better off not knowing.

On leaving to return to France, which I did on Thursday evening, my dear Ethel broke down completely. No one had written and told me how ill she had been. It was her cousin Herbert from Platt, who, when he came back from leave three weeks later, brought me something from her and told me how ill she had been. Well, I knew when I was home and with her that she was taking it hard. Having seen the partings between loved ones, at Victoria Station, when I was waiting to board the train for Folkestone, I really felt sick at having to leave her and my family. There were men like me waiting to return to the battlefield in France with wives and little children there, and they were all crying. On the Thursday evening, I had gone to London and stayed at the rest home in Waterloo Road overnight.

At the first opportunity, I got into a carriage, and I never looked out the window until we had left Victoria Station, it was too upsetting. I vowed then, however long I am away, if I am not killed, I will never go on leave again until I can go home for good. And that is exactly what happened.

I went back to Folkestone and had to wait until the evening to cross. We landed at Boulogne at 10.30pm and went to the rest camp to have a sleep. The next morning we left for Bethune, where we stayed at the stores. Today was my father's birthday. We then went to a place called Sally Labourse where the battalion was resting. I saw Fred, so we were now together again facing more duty.

Chapter 14

The next day we returned to the same reserve trenches that we knew so well. We stayed in reserve, covering for various regiments from our Division. The fighting had thankfully died down, and neither side seemed to have won much ground over the past six months. The British had gained a very small amount but had lost terribly in men and material. Of course, the Germans must have also lost a significant number of men.

By Easter Monday, April 24th, a Scottish Division had arrived to take over the sector that the 12th had been in. The chaps who served there reckoned it to be the worst place, other than Ypres that they had existed in. And that is what it was; in no way could it be termed living, it was purely surviving from one day to the next. The following day, the weather having turned Springlike, with the sun shining, we said good-bye to that sector and entrained at Noaux les Mines railway station to go to Lillers for a complete rest. The members of the Battalion, who had been involved in the fighting from the start, needed this rest badly.

Now let me go back a bit. What had we gained and what had we lost?

Well Corporal Cotter, of the Buffs, had died after being awarded the Victoria Cross for conspicuous bravery. In our Battalion, Lance Corporal Moon had been recommended for the Victoria Cross for exceptional gallantry in the face of the enemy. Charlie Moon had held a point on the line, which 'D' Coy was defending, on his own for twenty minutes before help arrived. Charlie was a bomber who threw Mills bombs, and when the officer and the rest of his group were either killed or severely wounded, he carried on alone, keeping the Germans away. He was immediately recommended by our Commanding Officer for the Victoria Cross. The Divisional General passed it on to Army Headquarters, and it was almost there. But was it? No officer had been there to witness and write about what Charlie had done. The officer in his party had been killed, and he had therefore been on his own. It was practically impossible to get a Victoria Cross or even a Distinguished Conduct Medal unless an officer had been present to witness the bravery. It would have been nice for the two Kent regiments to each have been awarded the Victoria Cross, but rules barred it happening. Captain Dawson had been awarded the DCM. This decoration was the first of his four awards for leadership and gallantry. He was now Commanding Officer of 'D' Coy and a fine officer he was too. Sergeant Hibbert had been awarded the DCM, and I believe that two or three more had been awarded, but I'm not certain of the names.

We had been through a very tough time since leaving the Armentières sector in November 1915, and had lost heavily in officers and men, not only killed and wounded but also through sickness caused by the terrible conditions under which we had to live. We had to stand-to at Allouagne, where we went after leaving the train at Lillers. It was feared the Germans were going to launch another gas attack as the wind was now blowing from the East. It didn't happen much to our relief, so we settled down in this peaceful village for a well-earned rest. On Sundays, we attended Brigade Church Parades where all four regiments of the 37th Brigade were drawn up making a square. The Padre conducted the service from the centre of the square. Our brigade padre had been the vicar of a Welsh parish and was well liked and respected by everyone. When we used to come out of those dreadful trenches in small parties, he would often be waiting on the road to give us a smile and a word of comfort. That was the sort of vicar he was.

We were able to go in small batches to the local Cinema. We had sports meetings, and in one race I actually came in first. In another race, Fred was third. The movies shown at the Cinema were in French, but we still enjoyed them. The weather was perfect and best of all; we were having much more food. I didn't have to go chasing after Fred all the time to supplement my rations. May came in, and to keep us fit we had Test Alarms and small marches, but we really were at rest as was all the 12th Division.

There were also Brigade Sports involving all the four regiments and us. The Royal West Kents won most of the prizes. We did well in the boxing too as our Champion had survived the war so far. We were entertained in the Theatre to concerts, and these were always well appreciated. We continued each Sunday to have the Brigade church parade.

All good things must come to an end, so we left Allouagne early in the morning on May 8th, marching eighteen miles to a place called Bony, which was a small village near Aire. Most of us ended up with sore feet, but we all finished the march. In addition, it was very hilly country, and there were plenty of storms around, but we were still well away from the front line. We, signallers, did a lot of flag work out in the fields and, all in all, we were feeling much better health wise. We didn't worry too much about what the future had in store for us; it was a stupid practice in wartime. We were all inoculated again as I suppose the first edition, which we had in Purfleet, had worn off. All through May, we continued to have drills and short route marches. Our numbers were continually increasing as drafts were added to us, some old hands returning and some new ones too.

June 1st, 1916 came, so the Battalion had been overseas in France for a year, and what a year it had been. On June 2nd the Battalion had an anniversary concert to celebrate our coming out from England a year ago. Captain Harris of 'B' Coy made a very sarcastic speech about the Battalion's work over the past year which practically everybody took exception to. He always had been very sarcastic, even when he was a junior officer. This man was the smart-ass officer who hadn't been around when the order had to be given to get the guns cracking when we were in those craters with the Germans almost up to our parapet. I almost felt like standing up and telling the chaps about it just get back at him after he made his sarcastic comments.

We were able to have baths regularly, and everything seemed to be going along fine. We began to wonder what was to follow as in the Army you never get something for nothing. On June 8th we bought the French Daily Mail and read of the tragic death of Lord Kitchener in the cruiser Hampshire. He was on his way to meet with the Russian leaders. This loss, in my opinion, was the most tragic thing that could have happened, for Lord Kitchener was, as Mr Churchill was in the Second World War, a symbol that people could pin their hopes on, and now he was gone forever.

We continued to have a lot of rain in June, and a new Brigadier had been appointed to 37th Brigade by the name of Brigadier Cator. On June 13th the Battalion attended a memorial service for the late Lord Kitchener in the hall at Allouagne. On June 24th our friend, Signaller Robinson, Robbo, went on leave to England and so missed the opening of the terrible battle which took place quite close to where we were. When Robbo came back, he told us that he had got married while on leave. We thought that he was totally daft. So many chaps went on leave, got married when they were on leave, returned and were then killed. Fortunately, Bert Robinson was the exception, for he stayed with the Battalion until the Armistice in 1918.

By June 26th we knew something big was afoot for we saw masses of troops marching towards the front line, including a troop of the Life Guards. Later on, the trenches had to be deepened for these men, especially the communication trenches, because of their height. As we approached the front line, the sound of continuous gunfire from our batteries became more pronounced. On the night of the 27th June, we moved out of this peaceful village and marched to a place called Flesselles, then on to a place called St. Gratien which was about nine miles away but much closer to the front line. We stayed here until June 30th. The weather was still very wet and the roads, as a result of all the rain and traffic, were very muddy.

We were soon on the move again to a place called Breche, which was about ten miles away and again closer to the front line. We were now pretty tired as we had been doing a lot of marching during the past few days. After a decent sleep, we were ready to go again.

On July 1st we set off at 5.00am to march a distance of three miles to a place called Millencourt. There we spent the day in a farmer's wheat field. We waited in full battle order for the instruction to advance, for, of course, the Battle of the Somme had commenced that day. That was the reason the sky had been alight now for a week with the flames from the guns on our side belching out shells, day and night. The British guns were almost wheel to wheel as far as the eye could see and there were stacks of shells the size of small houses waiting for the gunners to use them. My word, Mr Lloyd George had done his job well as Minister of Munitions for wasn't it only last November when Captain Towse had asked for a few more shells to be fired from the artillery, only to be told that because it wasn't an SOS, they couldn't fire any as they had a severe shortage of ammunition..

The wheat field that we were in was just off the main road on the east bank of the Somme River. Close to where we were waiting, there was a road junction where we could observe fleets of ambulances coming and going all day. The heat from the sun was intense, and we weren't able to sit down as the wheat was up to our waists. We weren't even able to use a toilet if indeed there was one available. We stayed in this wheat field until 7.00pm on that day of July 1st. I had seen Fred and Len Bush, so I knew that we were all in this together.

The ambulances stopped at the crossroads, which like a lot of other crossings throughout France had a crucifix, in a prominent position. This particular crossroads we were beside got the name 'Crucifix Corner' for obvious reasons and is now part of the folklore of the Battle of the Somme. Albert was about a mile down the hill to the right. The steeple of its church tower was hanging down having been hit by a shell. The noise of the guns, which were still firing, was intense as it had been for the past week. At night the whole sky was lit up with fire from the flashes of our guns.

We moved off as I said previously via Albert and at the end of the long communication trench, there were guides to take each company to its allotted position in the front line. Our guides were from the Rifle Brigade of the 8th Division which were to have taken Ovillers-La-Boisselle. The plan was that we would then advance as many miles as we could before nightfall. But nothing ever went as planned on our side. The Germans seemed to have had prior notice of the attack, and had reinforced their lines by positioning a new machine gun post every so many yards. They were positioned in such a way as they could pour merciless crossfire into no man's land where our troops had been trying to cross. The heavy machine guns that the Germans used were every bit as good as our Vickers-Maxim machine guns and always did their job.

Our guide took 'B' Coy up to the front line with Captain Harris as Officer Commanding.

'Here you are, Sir. This is your position,' the guide said, pointing to the nearest trench.

'But where is the company?' the Captain inquired.

We were looking around but didn't see anybody as it was a very dark night.

'You'll see them in the morning, Sir, when you are able to look into No Man's Land,' our guide told the Captain. He then left us to it.

And indeed we did see them in the morning. The men from that regiment together with men from other regiments were lying in lines as hay or corn would lie in a field, every one of them dead. They had all been mown down by those German machine guns. Every one of us couldn't believe the sight before us. How could such a massacre have been allowed to happen?

Breakfast time came, and as the chaps of 8 Platoon were eating, they heard movement in a small dug-out nearby. When they investigated, they found a young Irish soldier terribly injured. His stomach had been ripped right down the middle, and all his intestines were lying out on top of his body. Our doctor was fetched, but he wasn't able to do much to help him as it was a job for surgeons. Volunteers were soon available to help, as the chaps had forgotten about their breakfast now, and when a stretcher was brought, he was laid tenderly on it and carried as gently as possible to the rear and then to the hospital The doctor said that if he could get to a hospital quickly for treatment he stood a fair chance of recovering from his terrible injuries.

That day seemed very long and, although it was Sunday, the terrible shelling from both sides went on. Later that afternoon we moved back to a support trench to break the monotony. 'D' Coy was already there. I met my brother, and he told me that the parents of Captain Matthews had sent him out a bullet-proof waistcoat for him, but he didn't intend wearing it when we went over the top on the following morning which would be July

3rd. Captain Matthews had told Fred that he had a premonition that he was going to die tomorrow, waistcoat or no waistcoat. His thought process was; why wear chain armour which was an encumbrance and would hinder his movement when he was going to die anyway.

Fred and I talked together for a few minutes. We then shook hands and wished each other good luck for tomorrow. Much has been written about men saying goodbye to each other before going into battle; but we were brothers and the only sons of our parents and looking at what had happened to the 8th Division, our chances of survival looked very slender. We would probably die together as brothers.

'B' Coy went back up to the front line under cover of darkness. The guns never stopped shelling all night. We were all issued with a full day's ration's to cover tomorrow. Jack Webb and I, plus a new chap whose name I don't remember; he had only recently joined us as part of a new draft of chaps, were to be 'B' Coy's signallers, with me in charge. The Lance Corporal had been withdrawn by Sergeant Dale. It always seemed unfair, as happened on this occasion, to give us men who had just arrived in France and expect them to perform under fire in a battle like we were going to be in tomorrow. Being old soldiers now, Jack Webb and I found a dug-out on top of the ground under the parapet; it was just off the trench. We lit a candle which we signallers had to use at night to compose messages. We took out our next day's rations and polished off the lot, washing it down with water. We felt that if we were to die tomorrow, the rats, of which there were many, wouldn't get our grub. We had then to wait another three hours; we had eaten our meal at around midnight. Our poor newly arrived mate was petrified with fear, and there was nothing that we could do to help. We had a smoke or two to help pass the time, we talked about anything other than our present situation and gradually the time passed. After we had got back out of this, we met another new chap from 7 Platoon. He told us that while Jack and I were eating and talking, he had been lying petrified on his stomach on the bottom of the trench, too frightened to move. He listened to our conversation, and he thought us marvellous. We told him that we had just become used to that sort of situation as he must, and that was the truth. You can get used to almost anything if you try and there is no alternative.

Chapter 15

The Germans had got quite a lot of observation balloons down this part of the line. We had a few but not as many. There were also a few small aircraft flying on each side, and our chaps of the Royal Flying Corps used to try and set the German balloons on fire, making the occupants jump overboard and land using their parachutes. I always felt that this wasn't their only method of observation. They seemed to know the exact distances to our trenches, and I suspect that they used ordinance maps. However they managed it, their shelling was remarkably accurate.

We, the signallers, moved out of the dugout just before 3.00am summertime when the major offensive of July 3rd commenced. Summertime had been introduced in both England and France at the end of April. We found that part of 'B' Coy was already out in No Man's Land. We got up over the parapet and moved towards the German lines. We passed over many bodies of the 8th Division who had been killed on July 1st. I went over to the German trench, and there wasn't anybody else about, friend or foe. It wasn't light yet, but there was definitely nobody there. Feeling very vulnerable I went back a bit looking for Webb and the other signaller. Suddenly, the German machine guns went into action. We learnt later that they had been hiding in deep dug-outs with their demounted machine guns in safety while we shelled their lines. As soon as our shelling moved on to their reserve trenches, up came the Germans with their guns being raised on ropes like a lift. All they had to do was mount the guns on the emplacements which were already in place. They were then able to let fly and send the murderous waves of bullets which mowed everybody down. I was suddenly standing alone out in No Man's Land, with everyone else either killed, wounded, or, the few who were still alive, were flat on the ground. I could feel the bullets going past me and yet, miraculously, I didn't get hit by any. I quickly got down on the ground; I was still holding my rifle and telephone. Webb had the wire. I saw Captain Harris get up to try and advance again, but he was hit and toppled over dead. I crawled over to where Webb was, and together we crept nearer to the German trench. There we stayed with a few of 'D' Coy who hadn't gone over into the second line of German trenches with Captain Matthews. He was killed, as were Captain Barnett of 'A' Coy and the Captains of both the other Coys.

When daylight really broke there we were, Webb and I and those few chaps from 'D' Coy who had survived, tucked up right under the German trench against the wire. I was lying on the outside, trying, with Webb's help, to remove a bit of soil from under me. A German sniper must have seen me moving and aimed two shots at me. They hit my tin hat too high up and glanced off into the air. I lay very still to let him think that he had killed me. On my left lay, a chap badly wounded. He asked me to help him. I told him that I couldn't even save myself and to be quiet. Being in pain, he continued to move about, and he was soon killed by a sniper.

We stayed under that German trench all day and wasn't it a never wracking time. The sun blazed down, and yet we couldn't move at all. The evening finally came along, and it was getting towards dusk. We whispered to each other that as soon as it got dark, we would make a dash for our lines. Suddenly, about fifteen yards from where we were one of our chaps, who was lying closer to the German lines, got up in a kneeling position, put his rifle up to his shoulder and fired over me. I looked around and just behind me was a German soldier coming through the wire. Our chap had toppled him, and he was dead. We got up and bolted, as we thought, towards our lines. In fact, we were running parallel to the German line. We came to a deep shell hole, and we jumped into it. There was the Sergeant from 'D' Coy with us, and he told us that the wire that we could see was our wire; I disagreed with him and told him that it was German wire and we should wait. I told him that once it got dark, our side will start sending up vary lights. We can use these to guide us back to our lines. I did this, but as we went the chap who shot the German was himself killed when he got tangled up in our barbed wire trying to join the East Surreys. They were now holding the line that we had left that morning.

The rest of us got through the wire safely and were fortunately recognised by the East Surreys. How we survived that day I know not; it was a miracle. We were soon going to the rear. At our transport lines, we met a ration party from the Buffs with Len Bush in charge. He was pleased to see me as he knew that it had been the Queens Royal West Surreys and us who had gone into action that morning with the objective of taking Ovillers-La-Boisselle. We had done no better than the 8th Division and had failed completely. Our casualties that morning were around 400 out of the 600 who had gone over the top. One of our signallers, Corporal Buss of Smarden, told me that he had seen Fred sitting in an ambulance travelling to the rear with the wounded. It turned out that Fred had injuries to his legs and he was shipped back to hospital in Nottingham to recover. He was out of it for a while. His boss Captain Matthews had been killed and we, the Royal West Kents, had lost not only a fine officer but a gentleman. We would miss him as of course would Fred as they had grown quite close over the past year.

It has been stated by no less a person than Sir Winston Churchill that the casualties at that Somme Battle on the first day of July were 60,000 killed, wounded or missing and here we were again on July 3rd still losing men by the hundreds in our regiment alone. I had lost friends that day whom I had met in my time in the army and friends that I had been at school with. Still, the battle raged, and the barrage of guns kept firing shells at the German lines. As we now knew they had little effect on the Germans; they seemed to bounce off without any effect. When the shelling commenced, the German troops took cover in their deep dug-outs. As soon as the shelling ceased they knew that we would be attacking and they took up their defensive positions. They even dismounted their machine guns and brought them down with them. It was a simple matter to then haul them to the top again, mount them and start firing. What was amazing was that nobody on our side seemed to know that this is what they would do. It supposedly took our senior officers by surprise.

A few days later the East Surreys were able to capture the trenches that we had attacked with very few casualties. The Germans had withdrawn to new defensive positions which allowed them to straighten their line and make it even harder to attack. It was only after they moved back that the dug-outs were discovered. The dug-outs were four or five storeys deep into the ground, and all of them were built like fortresses. As I mentioned earlier, the stairways were made so that the machine guns could be hauled up by ropes with the guns standing on a platform. They could very quickly, once the shelling stopped, mount their machine guns and commence firing their deadly fire.

The men of the 8th Division, and others along the line who attacked that fateful July day had been told that the Germans would all be dead and all they would need to do was march across No Man's Land and occupy the trenches. Nobody on the British side thought that they could have survived a week's uninterrupted bombardment? When we heard of the large number of men that had been killed in the first three days of the Battle of the Somme we wondered why nobody had checked to make sure that the Bombardment had worked before Division after Division were sent to attack the machine guns.

The shelling hadn't even stopped them having hot meals as they had made kitchens at the bottom of all these deep dug-outs. They had been cooking full meals with a chimney running right up through the earth to the top to take the smoke away. The powers that be, Politicians and Generals, still thought that we could win the war with obviously outdated tactics. Us soldiers were capable of doing a lot better and of matching the Germans because we were good, but the Generals hadn't learnt the modern art of war. They were still playing at soldiers as they had done in South Africa against the

Boer farmers who went into battle on ponies. The Generals, called Donkeys by the Germans, still believed that the Cavalry was going to win the war. I leave you to judge the sanity of that idea.

We were relieved from our position and went into reserve in Blighty Wood, just behind the front line. On July 8th I was doing signal work around Crucifix Corner when I saw one of our small scouting planes flying very low. He was too low in a dangerous area, and, in front of my eyes, he was brought down by a shell from one of our own guns.

We were moved out of this sector into billets in Albert, and some other villages close behind the lines. The villagers were short of water and were also forbidden to sell us bread, so we existed on biscuits and bully. On July 12th I received a letter from Fred letting me know that he had been moved to a hospital in Birmingham and he was doing well. I was delighted that he was recovering as I had been worried about him. I also missed the extra grub he had always been able to get for me. It was in late July that Lance Corporal Moon was promoted Corporal and posted to 'B' Coy, that enabled me to see more of him. Nothing yet had been heard about the recommendation to award him the Victoria Cross.

We watched big drafts of new chaps going up to join many of the regiments which had suffered catastrophic casualties. So far, we had received no replacements in our own battalion. We required a bunch of new officers, with the exception of one who had survived. Nearly all had been killed and some of the others wounded. Captain Dawson had been wounded at the craters when he won his DSM, and so missed the early days of the Somme Battle. The Commanding Officer and the Adjutant were the only ones left. It was the Company Officers who had been killed.

Sometime around the middle of July, there was a rumour going around that His Majesty King George V was in France. We heard that he was inspecting the Royal Sussex Regiment which was representing the 8th Division, but we also heard that the Royal Sussex were down to around one hundred men and that included everybody from their Transport section. We also heard that fellows in the draft who were passing through the area on the way to other regiments were suddenly drafted into the Royal Sussex and quickly given new cap badges and numbers. They didn't want the King to see the true decimation of the regiment. Perhaps that was a mistake from our point of view, but of course, the Generals didn't want the King to see the full horrific picture.

So terrible was the loss of life in July that when we had a draft to help make up our numbers, we had chaps from five or six other regiments. Some were happy to stay with us and become West Kents, while others, wishing to get back to their mates in other regiments, were afterwards allowed to leave and rejoin their comrades.

On July 27th, after a while resting and doing fatigue work, we again went forward. This time we passed through the village of Ovilliers-La-Boisselle, whose capture had cost not only the 8th Division but also, our Division so many lives. The whole village was flattened to the ground as the result of our massive bombardment by the heavy guns, but the dug-outs were still there intact, deep and cosy and not harmed at all.

Our High Command hadn't yet worked out a way of stopping the Germans hiding away and then quickly emerging with all their machine guns to mow us British soldiers down like corn being reaped. We relieved the 49th Division which was the same Division that we had relieved in Plug Street Wood in June 1915.

I and others had been doing orderly work as we hadn't been able to get the telephones fixed largely due to our men being all over the place. Not having telephonic communication didn't stop the guns belching out fire and shells. The Germans were quieter than they had been at Hulloch and Loos. It was on July 19th that we found the spot where Captain Matthews fell. He, with some of 'D' Coy on that fateful day of July 3^{rd,} had reached and passed the second line of German trenches and his and the bodies of the men who were with him were all still lying where they fell.

Just before the Battle of the Somme commenced, it had been announced in orders that a new medal would be awarded to other ranks. The officers had already got the Military Cross in addition to the DSM, but other ranks only had the Distinguished Conduct Medal (DCM), which carried with it a small premium for life. Medals didn't worry us; however, at the end of July two stretcher bearers named Wells and Riley were awarded the new medal which was called the 'Military Medal'. Some others were given the medal too, but I personally knew Wells and Riley, so that meant more to me. They never pulled back from going over into No Man's Land

and getting in chaps who had been wounded and couldn't make their own way back.

We continued to stay in and around the trenches, from Crucifix Corner up to and around Ovilliers-La-Boisselle. I remember that we tried to have a bath in some ponds near Crucifix Corner but were shelled by the Germans who were now using light aircraft for observation purposes so as they could direct artillery fire.

By August 3rd we were ready for action again, but fortunately this time we weren't required. We went up in support of the Buffs and Royal Fusiliers. It always puzzled us, soldiers, what happened to the Germans who were killed, for never did we see a place marked by the enemy to denote that their dead were buried there as we did with our own dead.

We, the West Kents, who were in support of these other regiments found out why: for the Germans had been taken by surprise by the speed of the Buffs and Fusiliers and, as we were just behind them this is what we saw.

Dead German soldiers had been tied up in bundles of three; two one way, and the third in the opposite direction. These bodies were placed on trucks which were on a very light set of rails enabling them to be taken quickly to the rear. A senior officer told us that once the bodies reached the rear, they were cremated. This method of body disposal quickly removed any trace of how many of their men were being killed. This method of body disposal also explains why there are many acres of French soil occupied by British dead and there are very few German cemeteries.

Would it have been better for the world to have known the total cost in human lives that Germany suffered or were they so ashamed of what they had done to their own population in starting the terrible war that they wanted to hide the figures? The parents and loved ones left behind in Germany knew the terrible cost of the conflict as their menfolk never returned from the Eastern and Western fronts.

On August 4th, the second anniversary of the start of the war, the Buffs and Royal Fusiliers went over the top in front of Pojiers and were successful in capturing three lines of German trenches that morning. Although they captured a lot of Germans and sent them back as prisoners, they were only able to consolidate one trench. By the way, the German chaps taken prisoner never tried to escape they were always very thankful to now be out of the war. You could see from their gaunt faces that they were suffering just as much as we were.

The Fusiliers had suffered a lot of casualties in the attack and defence of the captured trenches, and it was the job of the West Kents to bury those chaps in the trench. There were plenty of souvenirs lying about, and I found a German Officer's diary, which I handed over to the Adjutant. There were also some views of a seaside place in Belgium where the German had been stationed. I still possess one of those postcards. It was on the afternoon of August 5th when the sun was shining brightly; we saw an incident that I am about to tell you now. We were in a trench which was on the side of a hill. From where we were, the valley stretched down and then went up again as it did all through the Somme battlefield. Below us and stretching up the other hill, were the Anzacs – the Australians and the New Zealanders.

Unbelievingly, we saw an Australian soldier, wearing his billycock hat, get up on to the parapet of the trench they were in, step out into No Man's Land, put his hands up showing that he wasn't armed. He then started to walk across No Man's Land towards the German trenches. No Man's Land was about three hundred yards wide at that point. In front of him, we could see a few trees that were pretty blitzed by shells. When he reached this spot, he stopped and then out of the trench came around 150 Germans; we were able to count them. The Australian Sergeant, we heard later that he was a Sergeant, got down into the trench and got a wounded man up onto the parapet. Putting the wounded man's arms around his shoulders, he managed to get him back to his own lines. During this whole heroic act, there had been perfect peace; not one shot had been fired by either side.

Suddenly, to the left of where I was standing and over the barricade of sandbags which had been erected in the trench, a German fired a volley up into the sky. Somehow I always felt that I should have said 'Thank you' soldier. This was the second time that we had been in the same trench as the Germans with only a sandbag barricade between us; but on each occasion, we respected each other and carried on quietly, both the Germans and us. We watched as German prisoners came up through our lines to the rear through the communication trench and we felt really sorry for them for most of them were in a bad state. To their credit, no British soldier said anything aggressive to the prisoners or made any actions towards them. Everybody understood that this was us, and our enemy and it could have been the other way around with us being the prisoners. We all knew by now what death and suffering meant, and it affected both sides.

Chapter 16

On August 6th, which was a Sunday, Sergeant Dale broke the news to his band of signallers that he had been appointed Quartermaster Sergeant of 'A' Coy and would be leaving them. We all wished him well and told him that we were sorry he was leaving. We genuinely were sad that he was moving on as he had trained us signallers from scratch. He had the knack of being able to pick the right chaps for the jobs that required courage and skill. He also seemed to be able to get things done to improve our comfort. To one and all he had been a friend and I know that I personally was sorry to see him move on. He had a wife and children at home, and as long as he remained a Signal Sergeant, he wouldn't get a promotion which included more pay.

I still received letters from Ethel, my parents, Fred and other friends, but with Sergeant Dale moving I felt very isolated and on my own. My brother had gone to recuperate at home, and so many of my friends had been killed, including Frank White, who came from Greenwich. I missed him as he had been a very nice chap and a very reliable friend.

We continued to do fatigues and were in and out of the trenches which by now were getting cleaned up with the dead finally being buried and the other rubbish being taken away. It is true that some ground had been taken from the Germans, but the promised breakthrough, which was supposed to justify the large loss of life, had not taken place. Far too many of the so-called new Army had been killed for no apparent reason.

On August 12th we watched our anti-aircraft guns bring down a German aeroplane. This was the first time that we had seen this happen. We, the British, were now using tethered balloons like the Germans for observation. One day one of our balloons broke free. Very soon there were about thirty of our small planes buzzing around it trying to get hold of it or shoot it down. Eventually, they managed to shoot it down, thankfully, after the observers had escaped by parachute. It was amusing to watch and broke the monotony.

On the night of the 12th, we were moved up again into the front lines. This time we were not going over the top but were just decoys so as the Germans would think an attack was coming from our direction. All the artillery fire from our guns was flying over our heads onto the German front lines, and our bomb teams bombed the German forward troops making them think that the attack was coming soon. In fact, it was our 35th Brigade, together with the Anzacs, who went over the top and, for once, were successful in taking all their objectives.

The next day was Sunday 13th August and clearing up parties were sent into the recently captured trenches. Our Corporal, Charlie Moon, was in charge of one party from 'B' Coy, and as he descended into a German dugout, he trod on a Mills Bomb that had the firing pin partly pulled out. Unknowingly, he released the pin, and the bomb went off blowing off one of his feet. He was taken back to the hospital where he later died. He still didn't know if he had been awarded the VC for his gallantry in March at the craters. Later on, we heard that he had been awarded the Military Medal. We lost, or more particularly, I lost a very close friend in Charlie, who was not only a fine soldier, but he always behaved like a gentleman should. I wrote to his parents at Southborough, and they wrote back saying that their youngest son, who was serving in the Royal Naval Division, had also been killed on the exact same day. They told me that the loss of these two sons meant that they had a total loss of four children in just three months. All the family that they possessed had been killed in this terrible futile war. See what war does; if your name is on the list to die, you won't be spared. That's the way we all felt anyhow.

I should have said that when Sergeant Dale left the signallers, Corporal Buss, one of the original signallers who had joined in August 1914, was appointed Sergeant. He didn't have enough experience in handling chaps and things soon began to get, what you might call, ragged. I'll tell you more about that later.

On August 19th we were inspected by General Scott who, as you are already aware, was our Divisional Commander. He not only praised us for what we had done on the Somme, but he also awarded a few Military Medals to some of those who had merited them. To many of us, awarding medals was all wrong, and I personally felt strongly about it. We agreed with the Victoria Cross for acts of extreme gallantry, but so many other medals were given to people who didn't deserve them.

Our next move was away from the Somme battlefield area towards Arras where at the moment the war was a lot quieter. We stopped at a sizeable village called Wailly which was about three miles from the town of Arras. We were all very pleased to get back to a quiet place which the war, as yet, hadn't destroyed. Wildflowers were growing on the sides of the trenches and in No Man's Land, indicating that there had been very little shelling recently. Everyone was put on fatigues carrying wood and other material into the trenches. We also did a stint on guard duty.

We were now an entirely different outfit than we had been a few months' previously. We had a new Commanding Officer called Colonel Owen. Our Adjutant, Captain Wingfield-Stratford had been promoted to Major and was now serving on the Divisional HQ staff. Our fine old Regimental Sergeant Major, who had set the discipline of the Battalion with fairness and kindness, right from the start, had left us to take up a commission in a Battalion back somewhere in the rear. Sergeant Dale, as already mentioned, had left the signallers, which was a big blow as he too ensured fairness and discipline for all. All our Company Commanders had also been replaced, and 'B' Coy now had a pleasant Commanding Officer, named Captain Williams. He was fair and held us signallers in high esteem. So many of the chaps had either been killed, wounded or were missing in action that 'B' Coy was composed nearly entirely by strangers. Tom Harris and all the other Halling boys had all gone, killed, wounded or simply ill; and so it went on. Fred had gone, and I was used to talking to him on a regular basis. Teddy Goose, with whom I had worked at Oxon Hoath in 1913, had been killed. Herb Ashdown was still an officer's servant in 'A' Coy, and we used to meet now and then.

In our new spot, the Germans used to bombard occasionally, mostly using what we called 'rum jars'.

These were very large mortar bombs and made one hell of a mess when they fell.

Now, very close to where 'B' Coy's phone was situated, there was a small party of technicians from Divisional HQ. They were using a newly developed instrument that was capable of picking up and interpreting the German messages sent over their phone lines. We, that is all the signallers, had been warned to only use the phone in emergencies as there was a fear that the Germans might have the same technology as we did. In fact, it later emerged that they had been using similar devices for a long time.

I obeyed the order to limit the use of the phone when I was on duty as I tried to stay out of trouble as much as possible. One evening the post had arrived at Battalion HQ. A chap named Spice, who was on duty at the HQ phone, rang me and told me that there was a parcel for me at Headquarters. I told him that I would get Bob Smith to pick it up later when he would bring 'B' Coy's report down. This chap on the HQ phone kept ringing 'B' Coy, asking for a piece of cake from my parcel. Each time my call number rang I had no alternative but to answer. This fellow kept ringing for a good long time. To make matters worse, Jack Wilson, who was on another Coy's phone, started ringing me too. These chaps got us into terrible trouble as we were reported to Divisional HQ for unnecessary use of the phones. The technicians were taking down a German message at the time, and the continual ringing of our phone interrupted what they were doing. It rather naturally made them very angry.

The next day we three signallers, who all came from 'B' Coy, were placed under arrest. We appeared before the Commanding Officer who now had Captain Alderman, formerly of the transport company as his Adjutant. These two officers were both long term professional soldiers and had no mercy. I was upset when the Commanding Officer didn't even allow me to explain my part in it. I was the unlucky one, and it was the other two idiots who had created the problem. I was keeping quiet knowing that the technicians were only a few yards from our telephone but of course, I had no option but to answer all the calls that came through on 'B' Coy's phone. All three of us were given ten days confinement to barracks and were returned to normal duty. Being disciplined meant that my signalling days were over. I wasn't too upset as, since Sergeant Dale had left, things weren't the same.

We packed our gear and rejoined our original platoons. Tug and I rejoined 8 Platoon. As I said earlier, we had new chaps now in all the companies. We were getting conscripted fellows, for conscription was introduced early in 1916. The new Sergeant immediately recommended me for a stripe as I was his most experienced man. He couldn't understand when the Company Sergeant Major refused his request on two or three occasions. When he spoke to me about it, I told him that the CSM didn't like me because of something that had happened earlier on in the war. Anyway, the Sergeant gave me a section to look after, and the lads were very grateful for my input because they were all new to it.

The CSM in question had joined at Maidstone, soon after Fred and I did. He had already been a soldier for several years. A little while before the war started, he had deserted over something. We were never able to find out why he deserted. He had been a Colour Sergeant in another regiment, but when war broke out, he had been picking fruit, etc. at a farm near Halstead close to Sevenoaks. The first time that he came on parade with us of 8 Platoon at Purfleet, Sergeant Pace, our South African War veteran, asked him' directly, why he had left the army. He had apparently seen that he was an old soldier as he knew all the drills better than Sergeant Pace. His answer was that he had been to New Zealand training recruits. Well, he soon got promoted and was made a Sergeant but he wasn't liked by any of us. He didn't ring true and seemed to be hiding something. When he applied for a free pardon, later on, it was learned that he had been a Colour sergeant in a regiment not connected with Kent. He went to France with us, and towards the end of 1915, when the existing CSM went ill, he was made CSM of 'B' Coy

When we were in the trenches during the awful winter of 1915/1916, they used to bring sandbags full of fuel, usually coke, up to the trenches when they brought up the regular food rations. The orders were that any of the coke that hadn't been used had to stay in the line even if we were handing over to another Coy. I and the rest of the chaps knew this rule existed. Well one day, sometime during March, we finished our stint in the trenches and were going back behind at Vermelles. Each company had two chaps who acted as runners: Bob Smith was one for 'B' Coy and a youngster, about eighteen or nineteen, had been given the job with Bob. Just before we, the HQ staff moved back, this CSM told this young lad to carry a bag of coke back to the CSM's billet at Vermelles, and he told him to get Kemp, me; to help him. Now, this is where the CSM made a mistake. Kemp had no intention of carrying anything back out of those trenches even if the Kid asked him to. I told the young lad; by this time the CSM had gone off as he always got out as soon as he could; that I wouldn't help carry the bag of coke. He had only carried it a little way when we came to a Vickers machine gun team.

'I say, Corporal,' I said to the man in charge, 'would you like a bag of coke that we have extra?'

'God bless you,' he replied. 'We were feeling really cold.

So the coke was handed over with the Corporal's blessing.

When we got to the end of the communication trench, which was about a mile long, we all had to wait and go down the road in small numbers. The CSM came to the back where we were and asked this young chap where the bag of coke was. The chap told the CSM that he didn't have it.

'Has Kemp got it them?' the CSM barked.

'No Sergeant Major,' the chap said.

'Where is it then?' he asked, none too gently

'Kemp gave it away to a Vickers machine gun crew.'

The young lad was shaking by now.

The CSM came over to where I was standing.

'Who gave you the right to give my coke away?' He shouted.

'And, what bloody right have you to take it out of the trenches when you know that it is forbidden,' I shouted back at him. He didn't frighten me.

When we got back to the billets, the CSM went and saw the Company Officer and both their names happened to be Harris. The CSM had enlisted under another name, but his real name was Harris. In fact, we had four Harris's in 'B' Coy. Still, let me finish up the story on the coke. The young lad was hauled up in front of Captain Harris, Officer Commanding 'B' Coy and was told to go and get me and then return to the line to get the bag of coke. I told the youngster that I would see them all in hell first. He began to whimper. I told him to dry his eyes and shut up.

We had been given an hour to bring it to 'B' Coy Headquarters. Well, of course, it was just a bit of trying it on, a fast one, but I wasn't having any of it. I told the lad to appear at the hour and tell Captain Harris and the CSM to go and fetch it themselves if they wanted it so badly. He was let off, and neither of the two bullies; for that's what they were, said one little word to me about it. You can see now why the Company Sergeant Major wouldn't give me a stripe when the Sergeant recommended me for one. But what did it matter, my primary objective was, as it always has been since, to do my best and try and stay alive. If I had been pulled up over the coke, I would have asked for a Court Martial. This punishment is what we signallers had been threatened with by the Commanding Officer when he gave us ten days confinement to barracks for the phone talking affair.

So here I was at the beginning again. News travels even in wartime. Fred was now in the Convalescent Camp at Eastbourne, and it wasn't long before he wrote to me asking for details about my return to the Platoon. A chap from 'B' Coy had gone home slightly wounded and was sent to recover in the same hospital as Fred. Let me add that neither the Company Officer nor the CSM with the same name was liked by officers or the other ranks. The officer because he was too cunning, and the CSM because he was a bullying coward. When you are in the thick of a war, you don't want their type of behaviour in addition to all the other trials we had to face.

Reflections - Chapters 13 to 16

The last four chapters can be summed up in the simple statement – A lot of fighting with microscopic gains and heavy losses.

You can tell from the tone of Sid Kemp's comments that he is becoming despondent. When he enlisted in August 1914, he did so along with his brother and a lot of men of his own age from the region in Kent where he was brought up. He was very fortunate in being selected to be trained as a Signaller; however, due to a nasty incident that he was blamed for he was returned to serve in 8 Platoon as an ordinary rifleman. I am sure that you have formed your own views on what occurred.

On returning to the Platoon, he found that he hardly knew a single person and, of course, they didn't know him. All the familiar faces had either been killed or wounded. When the Sergeant in charge of 8 Platoon wanted to give Sid a stripe, as he was the obvious person to lead and train the new arrivals, he was blocked from receiving it. The CSM had been shown up for what he was by Sid and, as a result, held a grudge against him. His brother having been severely wounded at the Battle of the Somme obviously also upset him. Fred had been sent back to England to recover, so Sid missed his brotherly chats.

He managed to get a week's leave although he was nearly prevented from being able to take that due to the process of selecting people for leave. The method of picking a man's name out of a hat was open to abuse and Sid was lucky that the friend of his, who was pulling out the names that day, didn't buckle under pressure from the other members of the Committee who oversaw the draw. They didn't want his name to be put forward for leave and wanted to change the rules to suit themselves. His Brother Fred's name came out of the hat on an earlier occasion, and he was stopped from going on leave because he was a member of the Headquarters staff. Fortunately, the officer he served, Captain Matthews, sent him on leave as part of the Headquarters team. It seems incredible that the Officers didn't get involved in choosing who went on leave as it was so key to the morale of the men. Getting a break at home, even just for a week, was an important event in a serving soldier's life and needed to be treated more seriously by those in charge.

Going on leave was quite an ordeal in itself. The fact that no provision was made to give the leave-takers clean clothes before they left France, and, also, they weren't provided with any food for the journey, meant that the short break from the front got off to a bad start. Sid had his last meal in France on Thursday evening and was only able to eat again on Saturday morning. He couldn't get out of his dirty, smelly clothes until he reached his home on Saturday. Returning to Flanders at the end of his leave seemed to be just as tortuous an experience.

In reading Sid Kemp's thoughts on the war that he was involved in, it is clear to see that he is getting sick and tired of the chaos that he is being asked to operate in. He is starting to question the little that had been achieved against all the friends he had lost. He and his colleagues are beginning to question the sanity of the decisions being taken by their superiors. He also doesn't like the attitude of a lot of the officers and the senior NCO's that he is in contact with.

I am sure that, based on what you have read, you are asking the question - Is it fair to blame the Generals for what is going on and the carnage of World War One? The simple answer to this issue is - Who else is there to blame as they were the decision makers and the men in charge?

Were the Generals merely a product of the system and shouldn't, therefore, be blamed or were they obeying orders from their political masters, especially Kitchener who had been Secretary of State for War?

Were their tactics wrong? They had minimum knowledge of trench warfare so how would they have known any better. The answer to all these questions is - Who cares, that is not the real point at issue here.

In the early war years, mothers, wives, fathers and other family members trusted their men folk into the care of the Generals, especially Kitchener who they saw as a hero who could do no wrong. Young, and not so young, men had volunteered because they felt that they had a moral obligation to do so. They didn't want to be branded as cowards, and anyway, it sounded good fun compared to their mundane existence at home. Those who enlisted saw going to war against Germany as being a big adventure.

The general public was led to believe that the people in charge were professional soldiers and therefore must know what they were doing. The belief at the time was that they would all be home by Christmas after giving the Germans a bloody nose. The big question that has to asked after the event is – "If they had known that

General French, and later Haig, believed that attrition was the only way to beat the Germans and win the war, would they have said that was acceptable to them? Did the trusting British Citizens agree that their men folk could be sacrificed in such vast numbers? The simple answer is – "No they didn't".

If the public had known, from the start, that their military leaders had decided the only way to victory was by allowing hundreds of thousands of their own troops to be killed, they would have said; "let the French get on with it, and we will defend our shores. The price that we are being asked to pay to drive the Germans out of France is too high. Sorry, Mr Frenchman but you are on your own".

The Generals didn't have the mandate to sacrifice those huge numbers of men just because they couldn't come up with an alternative strategy.

The politicians also had a responsibility; they should have reined the Generals in.

If you go to the battlefields and look at the names on the gravestones, they will cry out to you – "Why me? Why was I put through this? Why was I killed at the age of eighteen?"

At Mametz one hundred and fifty of the Devonshire Regiment were killed on the same day, in the same place and within an hour of each other. They were all ordered to advance and attack against a machine gun that was locked onto where they were leaving the trench. Surely it wouldn't have taken a lot of intelligence to stop the advance after the first two or three had been killed, take out the machine gun in question, and then resume the attack. The most likely scenario was that the officer in charge was one of the first ones killed.

When the BEF arrived in France, the Generals had a rude awakening. It was like taking a group of club members from London and sticking them in a hostile French countryside. In addition to the inconvenience, it was most unfair; the 'Boche' were shooting at their troops, and they were having to come up with instant solutions to the challenges they faced.

A notable fact was that the Generals were all in their fifties and sixties and used to a comfortable military life. Some of them had actually retired and were pulled back out of their retirement. Most of them had fought together in the Second Boer War and had served in other parts of the Empire together. They had established who they got on with and who they couldn't stand. They didn't want anything to do with the ones they disliked and were experts in ensuring that they were posted far away from them.

They solved problems by shouting and abusing those that they disagreed with. A lot of them were known for being easily annoyed and sent into apoplectic rages. Teamwork was not a word they knew much about other than in a game of Polo or Rugger. Rank over-ruled compromise, in fact, they didn't know the meaning of the word. Each one felt that they were right even when they had been proved wrong on a number of occasions. To admit you were wrong, they saw as a flaw of character. The fact that an offensive operation had lost six thousand men didn't indicate to them that they were doing something wrong. They were quite unused to using their brains to solve problems and arrive at new and different strategies. If Gordon had used it in the Sudan, then it was alright to use the same tactic now. Planning was a necessary evil and not an essential precursor to any offensive.

I would like to again refer to one of the most successful generals in the war, Monash, who built his offensives around excellent planning. He had a brain, and he used it. As I mentioned before he wasn't afraid to say "No Way" when he didn't agree with the orders he was being given from on high. If an English General had taken the same approach, he would probably have been fired and sent home in disgrace. That was the culture. If I am Commander in Chief then I must be right; there is, therefore, no need to take any other view into account.

If one takes Monash as an example, then it is possible to see that the war could have been run differently and, possibly with fewer casualties. The more likely scenario in the ranks of the British Military machine was that the General would say to his Division Commander; 'So get on and do what I say. Don't argue; I have just given you an order.'

If they suggested that the offensive mightn't be successful and that it should be postponed until certain things were corrected, they were told not to be a coward. Imagine the following:

'But Sir, the battlefield is a lake, and it is still raining. The guns can't be moved, and the troops can't attack through the mud. The roads and tracks that we use to bring the ammunition and food forward are no longer available; we can't even see where they were. There is no way I can achieve the objective you have given me.'

'You're a coward if you don't obey my orders,' the General shouts, red in the face with rage. 'If you can't do it I will get somebody else who can.'

'The slaughter will be very high: we will lose a lot of men.' The divisional commander adds.

'The Germans will lose more men than we will so it will all be worthwhile.'

'So despite what I have told you, you are saying that I must still attack. I want it to go on record that it is very unlikely that we will achieve any of the objectives we have been set and our losses will be very high.'

'I have given you an order now go and carry it out or, as I have already told you, I will get someone who can.'

To make things even more challenging, the infantry were instructed to carry a huge weight on their back as they carried out an attack. If they were shot, they would most likely pitch forward from this heavy pack. They would go head first into the mud and drown unless somebody pulled them out and turned them over. The other members of the platoon were banned from stopping and attending to the wounded; they had to continue advancing.

As we have read from Sid's account of the battles he was involved in, before any offensive, there was a heavy bombardment of the German positions. As already described this had little effect on the Germans manning the trenches. They had deep dugouts where they sheltered. As soon as the bombardment stopped, the Germans emerged from their cover and were ready to defend against the attack.

On the occasions where there had been heavy rain, the bombardment created more mud and deep craters filled with water; this made it practically impossible for the attacking infantry to advance.

The field commanders, for the most part, knew whether they would succeed or not. Unfortunately, in most of the army corps, there was no consultative process, so their views were seldom taken into account.

Ground rules and strategies were developed for use across the BEF with the intention of minimising losses. In the more successful attacks, these were followed, and the right level of planning was carried out. In most offensives, the rules were ignored because, early in the attack, things started to go wrong and delays occurred. As we have seen in Chapter 9, this could be anything from torrential rains to traffic congestion. Troop movements in a lot of cases were delayed, i.e. the Canadians at the Battle of Loos. Arriving late meant that the attacking troops didn't know their new area and hadn't had time to knock out key hostile machine gun positions.

The result of these delays meant that losses were much greater than expected. As mentioned, General Monash didn't attack until everything was in place as per the agreed plan. His losses were a lot less as a result of his strict adherence to what had been agreed. Haig tried to get rid of Monash on a number of occasions because he was showing him and some of his principal commanders in a bad light. General Smith-Dorrien had proved himself to be a good General, but he wasn't a "Yes" man when he knew that orders he had been given were wrong. General French had him sent home because he was too good and showed him up - Pathetic.

The War is like a two sided picture. On the one hand is the action side. The trenches, the first aid stations, the supply lines, the gun batteries, the tanks, the feeding stations. Action, action, action – death and destruction and no relief from the horrors of war. High level of noise and shelling. There was no use in worrying – if you were alive, you hadn't been hit yet. If you were hit, then your life ended, or you were shipped home.

On the second side of the picture is a chateau occupied by high-level officers. They all look the same and are all roughly the same age, 55 to 65. Same moustaches, Uniforms matter as how you look tells everybody how important you are. They are all warm, dry and well fed. Rank is the key to relationships. They are all 'prickly' with one another. If you have crossed swords with another officer ten or twenty years previously, then they are an enemy for life. You certainly wouldn't have them reporting to you. You only want 'Yes Men' on your staff as you don't want to have to explain or justify your decisions. You get loss figures on a daily basis, and you know that the numbers have probably been doctored downwards by your subordinates so as not to upset you too much. You can get in a nasty rage if you get upset. All the bad stuff is happening twenty miles away, so it is bearable. You get annoyed when a politician visits and doesn't think that you are marvellous and doing a great job. It is irritating when they tell you that you are not achieving anything and you are still losing staggering amounts of manpower. Do they not know that there is a war on and people get killed in wars?

It is hard to believe that in 1815 Wellington defeated the French at Waterloo with casualty figures of twenty thousand men. In 1914, here we were entering a war on the French side because of a treaty, drawn up by politicians. A million casualties later the allies had partly won the war, and twenty years later there was another massive war where the UK had four hundred thousand killed in action.

Chapter 17

Back to Sid who is at a place called Wailly, between the Somme Battlefield and Arras.

The reserve trench we were now occupying was adjacent to a road which was now part of the war. Just beyond where we were stationed was a canvas curtain hung across the road. Beyond this makeshift curtain was open space which led up to the front line. German snipers were on the lookout for targets on the road which was the reason for the curtain. I, with a few others and the 8th Platoon Sergeant, were on guard at this curtain to stop anyone from passing this point. Very few people wanted to get killed, so we didn't offend anybody by asking them to nor go any further. I was doing duty one day when walking up the road came General Scott and his Aide. I recognised the General from the Inspection Parades that he had held.

'Good morning sentry,' he said. 'We just want a look at the land up to the front.'

'Right Sir,' I said, but I didn't salute.

After several minutes they came back.

'Thank you, sentry,' he said. 'We have observed all we need to see.'

Now we had all seen and met General Scott quite a lot since General Wing, the 12th Divisional Commander had been killed last October at the Battle of Loos, and I knew that he was our Divisional Commander. A few minutes later the sergeant of the guard came along.

'Everything quiet?' He asked.

'Yes,' I said, 'but a little while ago General Scott came by. He wished me good morning, and he went up the road towards the front.

The Sergeant frowned a bit. 'But why didn't you call out the guard?' he asked.

'Well,' I told him. 'It was just a personal visit, and he didn't want any fuss.'

You see, even in war, you could enjoy bits and pieces and ordinary moments. The trouble seemed to be that those in authority so often forgot there were other human beings as sensible as themselves, even if we were only Tommies. Incidentally, I never liked saluting anyone throughout my life in the Army and didn't do it if I could get away with it. Call someone 'Sir', yes; as I still do. The word 'Sir' attached to anything that you are addressing to someone sounds much better than using Christian names as has become the custom now.

We stayed in this quiet sector of the line working and doing the trench work until September 27th when we were relieved by the Rifle Brigade of the 14th Division. We then returned to the Somme battlefields. We had a draft of about two hundred join us from England; they were mostly conscripts now. We travelled on buses and then marched down through Albert, Fricourt and Trones. Trones was where a handful of the 7th Royal West Kents had held off a heavy German attack for a whole day the previous July. They hung on until they were relieved in the evening by reinforcements. These fellows, some of whom were Sevenoaks chaps were under the command of Captain Anstruther, who, like Captain Dawson, was a Junior Officer at the depot in Maidstone when war was declared.

By October we were stationed on land that had been so dearly won close to Fleurs. We had to sleep out in the open.

Early in the morning on October 1st I was up early having a wash and a shave when I couldn't believe my eyes. Coming out of the mist were three huge machines which I later learned were tanks. These, together with one more which tried to span a sunken road and fell between the banks, were the first military tanks ever to be used in warfare. It appears that they had been sent up in the early morning to frighten the Germans. When we went up to the front line later, we couldn't see what they had done other than to leave one behind which the German artillery was using for target practice.

We went forward and were in the front line with the New Zealanders, but these were withdrawn shortly after we arrived.

October 3rd was Fred's birthday but, of course, he was still over in England recovering from his wounds. The weather was becoming colder now, and the only place that we had to sleep was on the floor of the shallow trenches. The guns on both sides never stopped belching out fire and shells, and both sides seemed to have an unlimited supply of shells for once. To make our misery complete, we had a lot of heavy rain, and this was very nasty at times.

On October 6^{th,} 1916 we moved over to a village named Guillemont which had been gained recently with the loss of great life. We were in position to go over the top once more. The trenches were very shallow, so we dug them deeper to be able to sit down without making our heads a target for the Germans. They were again entrenched on the side of a hill as they had been at Ovilliers in July. There was a valley between us.

On the morning of the next day, October 7th, we were quietly talking when out from No Man's Land came a lone German soldier. He put his hands up in the air and shouted 'prisoner'. The chaps were guiding him to the rear when he suddenly put up his hands over his head and kind of signalled to the German lines. We wondered if he had been sent to see what state of readiness we were in and whether we were getting ready to attack. If they had that information, then they could get their machine guns in position again. Alternatively, he may have just been waving to his mates.

This time we were to go over the top at 2.00pm.

'B' Coy, which I was part of, was scheduled to be the last to go. We watched in horror as those in the first attacking companies were mown down in front of our eyes by the German machine gunners. 'B' Coy started to go down that valley of death with three Platoons already gone and most of those now dead. When the Commanding Officer saw the massacre, he sent Corporal Tom Aspinall, of the signallers, to tell the officer to stop 8 Platoon going over.

Tom shouted, 'for Christ's sake don't go, the Commanding Officer has said that you must not go.'

Well, I had just left the trench and was at the top of the little parapet, about to go down into that valley of death. I darted back and took refuge in the trench. Our Battalion had been decimated again without any possibility of the objectives being attained. When would the powers that be learn their lessons so as the carnage could be reduced?

The Buffs, on our right, were also practically wiped out and they again lost their Commanding Officer. He, like the previous one who was killed, always led his men into action. Our Commanding Officers directed operations from behind. Some more of my signalling friends were killed. Bill Norburn and his companions Mankelow and Moffat were trying to lay wires before the trenches were taken. They in August had been given ribbons of the Military Medal. Neither they nor anybody else knew what for, but they were nice chaps, and again I ask, why are some singled out to be given presents when every man was giving their best in that horrible war?

After that carnage on the afternoon of October 7th it seemed as if we, the Royal West Kents, had been sacrificed to enable our brother Kent regiment, the Buffs, take their objective, but like us, with terrible loss of men. Before we went into action, I mentioned that we had received a lot of new drafts to make up our numbers. These drafts of men were young conscripts who had been taken into the Army at eighteen years of age under the Military Service Act, which introduced conscription. This Act came into law early in 1916, and most of those that had joined us in 'B' Coy came from the eastern counties of Norfolk and Suffolk. After our Commanding Officer had stopped 8 Platoon from going over the top, we settled down in the trench to wait; we had been warned not to attempt to try and return from the front line via the Communication Trench, even to get the wounded out. The Germans put down a very heavy barrage on the road leading out of the front line trenches.

About 3.00pm the Germans duly started shelling closer to where we were and gradually appeared to box us in, that is, those of us in 8 Platoon. For four hours all we could do was sit and endure it and hope that they didn't drop one into the trench, we were in. This bombardment was the worst that I had ever been subjected to. Later it was stated that this was a new technique being used by the Germans called a box barrage. They would select a party or section in a given area and carry on banging away at it until it was wiped out. I smoked a pipe in France, and all I could do was continue smoking while talking to a new Sergeant, who was decidedly windy, and to Fred Lambert from Halling, one of only a few left from the original 8 Platoon. All we could do was wait and wait. One youngster died, I should imagine from a heart attack for he wasn't hit. Later on, we missed the Sergeant and found that he had somehow slipped away and got to a field dressing station. I never saw him wounded, but all along I knew that he was scared stiff. Later that night we were relieved by the Queens Regiment and went back to the support line.

The following night we returned to the trenches to carry out badly wounded Buffs, and there were lots of them as well as quite a few dead. The journey back out of the trenches was a long one. When we got near the end, we came across the Royal Medical Corps' chaps who helped us on the rest of the journey to the rear. We carried ours down, I and three others, and were just kipping down in the support trench when we were called to carry out some of our own regiment; this time to the ambulances. Lying on a stretcher, waiting to be moved, was Signaller Spice. He was one of the chaps who had been involved in the telephone ringing affair which had caused me to be moved back into the Platoon a few days earlier. He was severely wounded in the legs and insisted to the Medical Corp's chaps that I, his mate, should carry, or help to carry him to the ambulance. I heard later that they had to amputate his leg when he got to the hospital. That was another signaller that I knew had left us.

We continued to live on the ground gained during the Battle of the Somme. Sometimes living in a blown up trench and sometimes living out in the open. We were not shelled too much at this time by the Germans which gave us some relief. The fire was being directed more at the front line. We went up once more to dig a trench for the Newfoundland Regiment of Canada. To have some sort of chance of attaining their objective, they needed to bypass the British Tank I referred to earlier which lay helpless in the middle of the sunken road, blocking it.

We stayed in and around the Somme until October 21st. The weather was now getting very wet and cold. We had regular rum issues and were also given a second blanket. On the afternoon of October 21^{st,} we packed up ready to leave the Somme. For me, as it turned out, it was for good.

We travelled in French buses driven by coloured chaps from Madagascar. We went via Amiens and Doullers to Bernville, which took seven hours to complete. We then had to march for three hours which brought us into the Arras sector of the front again. The next day being a Sunday, we slept late and were then inspected by our Commanding Officer.

A couple of days later we found ourselves back at Wailly, the place where we had been stationed before we left for that last battle at the Somme. What had been gained by all that terrible loss of life of young British manhood in the Somme battles? Was it done to help the French who had been battling since early Spring to try and keep the Germans from capturing Verdun? The French army was said to have suffered terrible losses, and perhaps the Battle of the Somme was to take some of the Germans away from that attack. Or was it, as some of the chaps used to say - 'When enough of us have been killed the war will have to end and the Generals don't know how to finish it in any other way.'

Well, it took another two years of terrible fighting before the Armistice was signed and we felt that nobody really won.

We stayed in and around this quiet part of the line doing trench duty and fatigues, for, of course, I was now back as a Private with 8 Platoon. I showed the chaps how to catch the large rats with wires. Some of these large rats were almost as large as a rabbit, and our food had to be kept hung up in the dugouts or else the rats would eat it on us. We and the rats had learned to live together, and I never heard of anybody being bitten by a rat.

On November 7th I was warned, with a few more of 'B' Coy, to pack up and be ready to move back away from the trenches. We had been chosen to work with the Royal Engineers at the railhead at Laboret. I have often wondered why CSM Harris chose me as one of the guys to go away from 'B' Coy. Perhaps it was to get rid of me so that I wouldn't expose his cowardly past to the new chaps. Still, I didn't gain very much by leaving the battalion in this quiet place. Our West Kent party was joined by parties from the three other Regiments of our Brigade. I should say about twenty chaps from each regiment joined us.

The first job was to erect tents to live in, and we were told that our duties were to help unload railway waggons of timber and other materials. On the evening of the 10th, when all except I and another chap from my tent were on guard duty at the Headquarters, we heard the sound of a low flying aeroplane, and we then heard the swish of a bomb falling. I saw it coming by the fire coming from it. The two of us were trying to light a fire at the time in a brazier in the tent as the other chaps had done in theirs. I threw myself onto the floor of the tent and, almost instantly the bomb exploded about eight feet away from the tent. The other chap was killed by the flying metal as he had remained standing. Those in the adjoining tents were either killed or wounded. The following day when the gunnery experts came to have a look at the bits of the bomb that were scattered around, they couldn't believe that I was still alive since I was practically under it when it fell. I think that it was the side of the tent that saved my life for it was riddled with holes from the bursting bomb. Our rifles, which were hanging in the tent, had their butts pockmarked by bits of shrapnel. The German pilot had also dropped another bomb on the Headquarters Guard post, killing the sentry and wounding or killing the others who were in the hut. Altogether six were killed that night, and eight were wounded. It was not a very happy start for our new team. A day or two later we went to a cemetery at Humbercamps where we dug the graves for our comrades and buried them with the Chaplain conducting the service. One of those was a chap called Turner who I had palled up with. We still worked on the railhead unloading wood and other materials which the Royal Engineers used or which they sent by carts drawn by horses to the various places in and around where our Division was now stationed.

Ethel's birthday had been on November 24th. I hadn't been able to send her anything but kept receiving letters from her and from my parents and friends. After the bombing, we had left the tents and gone to live in the huts occupied by the Royal Engineers.

On December 12th, the Germans, having observed a lot of activity at the railhead, had brought up an armoured train as close as possible to their front line and had started bombarding this railhead with large shells. In the course of the shelling, they hit the hut occupied by the Middlesex Regiment. We had groups from all the regiments in the Division now working at the depot. Several chaps from the Middlesex Regiment were killed and several more wounded. The Germans continued to fire shells over for several nights, and we found it safer to take to the fields during the evening rather than stay in the huts and be killed. We again had to go and dig graves for the chaps of the Middlesex Regiment and attended their funerals. We completed the job by filling in the graves. The losses at the railhead were becoming worse, so we were told to pack up our belongings and march back to our depot at Beaunute. Later, on December 16^{th,} we joined up with the battalion again; they were at rest. To me, this felt like a new battalion as nearly everybody was a stranger to me. We were still expected to play football in the afternoon, one Platoon against another. Playing team games seemed an attempt to create teamwork and inspire us with confidence in each other, but these chaps were total strangers, and it was hard to change that by simply playing football together.

We continued to stay out of the trenches, playing football or simply watching. We were now at a place called Sonbuin where there was a theatre, and everything possible was being done to cheer people up. The new boys were ill at ease, and the few old 'uns were also getting a bit fed up with the way that the war was going and the fact that there was no sign of an end. A year had passed, and Christmas was here again, but a lot of the people who had been with us last Christmas were now dead. Christmas Day to me was just another day. True there was plenty to eat, and we even had some beer, but I was glad when night came. I went and lay down and slept and tried to forget.

Chapter 18

Now let me go back a bit. In the Autumn of 1916, after I had returned to the Platoon, we suddenly found out one day that there were no potatoes for dinner. We heard later that there had been almost a very poor crop of potatoes in England and, in addition to that, the potato crop in Ireland had totally failed. As there were plenty of sweet chestnuts growing in France, we were fed boiled chestnuts with our dinner for several days. We were never overfed when we were in the army, so we got used to going hungry. The potato crop failure boded badly for the potato crop for 1917 as the larger seed potatoes would be eaten. After I came home to England in 1917, my parents told me that it was true about the potato failure of 1916 and that everyone was saving the small potatoes which usually they boiled up and fed to the pigs and chickens. They had to plant these small ones the following Spring.

After a few weeks, we in France were being fed potatoes again, but the bread shortage was getting serious, not only with the army but also in Britain too. I remember after I had returned to 8 Platoon, being asked to cut a single loaf into sixteen slices. As I did it, I was being watched, vulture-like, by the new conscripts. They were making sure that each slice was the same thickness. I always had the last slice, and often it was the thinnest of them all. How I missed my brother now, for when he had been the servant of Captain Matthews he was able to pass me on food not required by the officers. But why worry, we went to war to win, and here I am moaning, no, not moaning reader, bloody hungry and fed up.

We stayed out of the trenches until the end of 1916 and, in fact, into 1917. On January 3rd I was selected, with some others, to do Battalion guard duty and the Regimental Sergeant Major said that we were the cleanest and tidiest guard that he had inspected for a long time. The reason for this was probably because our guard was made up mostly of old soldiers who had pride in everything we did.

On January 4th, I, with some others, was picked out to go further to the rear of the line to form a Base Depot. Football was still being played by the Companies and Platoons in reserve, and also drills were the order of the day. On January 10th we, who were to form the Base Depot, were inspected by the Commanding Officer and passed as suitable for the job. I, at last, received a letter from my brother Fred. He had recovered from his wounds and was back in France at the base at Etapes. He was sent from there to the 1st Battalion, so we didn't meet again while I was in France.

By January 10th the first snow of the winter fell, and I began to feel unwell; however, I didn't go on sick parade and tried to keep going. Well the party, who were to form Base Depot, left the rest of the Battalion at Sombrin on January 12th and marched to Liencourt where we were to be stationed or where we thought we were going to be stationed. Just as we settled, we were told to move off once more, and we marched to a place called Hautecourt which was closer to the front line. The weather was turning very cold now with snow falling regularly. There was also a hard frost at night. It appeared that we at the depot were there to be drilled and smartened up for when we would return to our

Regiments. Our role was to encourage and train the new boys who now were all conscripts. Fred wrote to me to let me know he was now back at the front.

On January 27th I was feeling so unwell that I had to go on the sick parade. I had felt rough many times during my time in France, but this is the first occasion that I had gone on sick parade, so I was bad.

I was given light duty, but by January 29th, I wasn't any better, in fact, I was worse, so I went on sick parade again. I had several boils on my left leg. The weather was bitterly cold, with intense frost both by day and night. We were presently billeted in huts with two tiers of bunks, and I remember that I used to put my water bottle under my head before lying down to sleep and use this water to shave with the following morning. That was the idea anyway, but in fact, the water was frozen in the morning despite me having lain on it all night.

I continued to go on sick parade as I wasn't improving, and was finally sent off to see the doctor. He was at a casualty clearing station which was under canvas. One boil on my left knee was so large that the doctor lanced it and the dressing was put on by an Indian orderly. Remember this fact for later in my story when I will tell you why I connect this Indian orderly with what happened to me afterwards.

Life was becoming very hard for me. Not only was it very painful to walk and to do the fatigues and drills, but the weather had turned into a bitterly cold winter. On February 7th, we were told to pack our belongings as we were going to rejoin our regiments. We of the Royal West Kents marched to a place called Agnes, which was a distance of about six miles, and there we were accommodated in huts to await the return of the Battalion from doing a spell of duty in the trenches at Arras. When I saw the chaps of 8 Platoon, almost everyone was a stranger to me. By now I was feeling decidedly ill. The Battalion was put on daily working parties, spending all day in front of Arras, or should I say behind Arras, helping to build up the railway and roads and other work. All this work indicated to us that there would probably be another major offensive in the Spring and it would be centred on the Arras battlefield.

Well, that is exactly what happened, but I wasn't there, but I did hear that the loss of life was again very heavy. I went on a march to work, and I was feeling pretty terrible now. In fact I too ill to work and had to lie down under a straw stack while the other fellows worked. I had now got a terribly hard lump coming up in my groin, and it was extremely painful.

Well, on February 19th, I reported sick to the doctor of our battalion. He immediately ordered me to go to the sick bay, saying that I had a septic thigh. Well, I stayed under the treatment of the MO for a couple of days; however, I was getting worse and not better.

On February 12th the doctor sent me by ambulance to the 38th Field Hospital. The medical officer there got his information from a medical card pinned to my jacket, for I was now being carried on a stretcher everywhere as I couldn't walk. This MO asked me my age and told me that he doubted if I would recover from whatever I was suffering from. I would be twenty-six years old if I survived to my next birthday which was on April 6th next.

I was passed further down the line to another casualty clearing station and then again moved further back, still in agony, until I got to the No. 6 Stationary Hospital at Frevent. There I was put in a tent with other patients. The date was now February 14th. The next day I was admitted to No. 5 ward of the hospital, and I was put in a decent bed which was something I hadn't seen for some time. To try and resolve the problem with my groin, I was operated on at about 3.00pm that afternoon. I was told later that poison had somehow got into my lymphatic system which passes from the foot to the brain. How I had been poisoned no-one seemed to be able to tell me. When I thought back, I remembered that my parents had sent me a new sort of stuff to rub on my body where the lice used to feed and breed. The ointment was supposed to reduce the lice problem. Previously we had been using a milder sort of stuff to try and keep the lice under control, but it hadn't worked on me. This new ointment that my parents had sent me was supposed to be much more effective. I used to scratch myself from the effects of the lice until I was raw. I reasoned that I must have created a situation where the poison meant for the lice entered my body at my groin. Solving one problem had caused another which was much more severe.

Well the operation, being relatively straightforward, was successful. To give it a chance to heal I was ordered not to get out of bed for any reason for at least seven days. On February 23rd I was allocated to go by Hospital train from Frevent to the base at Etaples, a journey which ended up taking around ten hours. We were given food and drink on the Hospital train, and it wasn't a bad experience now that the pain had been reduced. We were also in much more comfortable surroundings which made me feel a lot better on its own. The appalling conditions that I had endured for the past few years had taken their toll on my health.

My brother had not stayed many days at the base before he was sent in a draft to rejoin the 1st Kents in the line. A few days after he joined them, a raid was organized to attack the German lines. He was waiting in a trench, with the rest of his party, when the Germans sent over a few whizz bang shells. One fell in a trench near to where he was waiting. He was seriously wounded again, this time in his left leg around the knee. Well, Fred survived and was sent to a field hospital where he was operated on, and he was then shipped back to England. This time he was sent to the Military Hospital at Epsom in Surrey. When my parents heard that he was at a hospital in Epsom, my mother, together with Ethel, went to visit him. They entrained at Wrotham Station and went to Victoria. When their train arrived at Victoria another train bringing men on leave from Flanders pulled up on the adjoining platform. Ethel and this is what she and my mother told me later, left my mother standing there, and went over to look for me amongst the soldiers who had just arrived. She said afterwards that she had heard me continually calling her name. In the end, she gave up looking, but still said to my mother 'I know that Sid was on that leave train because I heard him, but I couldn't find him.

They went on to Epsom to see Fred. When I was able to write to Ethel and tell her that I was in hospital after an operation, she was able to establish that the day of my operation was the same day that she was convinced that I was on that leave train. She was so convinced that she had heard me call her name that she had hunted through all those soldiers getting off at Victoria Station. Up to that point, I had even told her that I wasn't well as I didn't want her to get worried. Well, that is something that I cannot explain, but Ethel and I loved each other dearly.

Now let me return to the hospital in France. The hospital at Etaples, where I was being treated, was staffed by doctors and nurses who had volunteered to come over to help from Boston in the USA. Now the doctor could recommend that a specific soldier could be sent back to Blighty, but all his recommendations had to be passed by the Commandant who was a British Officer Doctor. Well, the doctor attending me felt that I would never recover fully from what I had suffered and I should be sent home. Incidentally, the doctor in the field station had also told me that it would take a long time to get better and I would be lucky to survive. The Doctor and Sister at the hospital that was treating me recommended that I be sent home to England. When the English top man came along to review my case he firstly asked me:

'How long have you been out in France?'

'Two long years,' I replied.

'My personal opinion is that you will get better soon and you had, therefore, better stay here in France. I am not agreeing to the request that you be sent home.'

In the next bed to me was a young Canadian soldier with a slight cut in his back from shrapnel and it was nearly healed.

'You can send this one to England,' the autocratic doctor said. 'A rest in England will do him good.'

This young lad from Canada had only spent about three months' service all told in France.

After the ward inspection was over, the Sister from Boston came and sat on my bed and cried. 'Don't cry Sister,' I told her. 'I am going back to England one day.' She marvelled and said that fellows back home in Boston would have gone raving mad.

'But Sister,' I told her. 'I am very fortunate to have survived as far as this. I have lost most of my friends, and they will never go home.'

She was, as were all the other doctors and nurses in that ward at No. 6 Stationary Hospital at Etaples, just the tops.

The early part of March I spent in bed having treatment. I began getting some letters from home after a period without any. In one of those letters, I was told that Len Bush had been taken prisoner during a raid by German troops on the Buffs lines. He had been wounded during the battle of the Somme last August, and he too had recovered back in England. He was held as a prisoner of war until the Armistice when he was released. He lived in England until he was seventy-one years of age when he died.

After the wound from my operation had healed, I was sent to see the Commanding Officer of the hospital and was marked down to go to a local convalescent camp. After a few days at this camp, I became very ill again. This time I had got a fever as well as my other troubles. This fever was later surprisingly diagnosed as Malaria, so back to hospital I went. This time I was placed in the

24th General Hospital which was also at Etaples. I stayed there first of all as a bed patient and then as I got better, as a help on the ward, assisting the Sister. I was feeling a lot better, so the doctor marked me to return to the Base for the Royal West Kents. Again, unfortunately, or fortunately for me, the morning before I was due to leave I was put on a fatigue helping to tidy up the reception hut, and, if required, to help carry new cases to the wards. Well, another chap and I had just one stretcher case to carry, and we did other work until knock-off time. I was feeling pretty bad. The ward sister didn't start until the evening. When she looked at me, she took my temperature and immediately sent notice that I would not be leaving in the morning as arranged. I was suffering from a high temperature caused by a fever.

The next morning the doctor examined me and immediately marked me down to be sent back to England. A few days later, on April 24th, I left France, travelling from Calais to Dover on a Hospital Ship. I was able to sit up on deck as it was a lovely day with bright sunshine. When the white cliffs of Dover came into view, I could have cried for joy. There were many times during my service in Flanders when it seemed to be impossible that any of us would survive.

On arriving in Dover, I went by hospital train to Brighton where I was placed in a hospital at the top of Elm Grove which overlooked the racecourse. This hospital had been a workhouse prior to the war.

The next day, after I had been examined by a doctor, I was weighed and didn't quite make nine stone. Before I had left Aldershot at the end of May 1915, I had weighed eleven and a half stone, which today is still my weight. I spent three happy months in Brighton. The people of that town were so kind and understanding, and they had many 'boys in blue' at the hospitals. We were given free rides on the buses, free seats in cinemas and theatres, free entrance to the piers and often, yes often, these kind and generous people of Brighton would buy cigarettes or sweets and then hand them out to the chaps who were walking or sitting on the sea front. I said earlier that I met Gus Ball on my first visit to the sea front and he was the only one from my Battalion that I met there.

In August 1917, I was sent to the Convalescent Camp at Summerdown, close to Eastbourne. I worked in the stores there for a while, checking linen, etc. A year previously Fred had been at the same camp, and he had told me at the time that he had done light duties to help. I left Eastbourne early in October, being signed off by a doctor who had to get everybody fit, at least on paper. I had ten days sick leave at home and then rejoined the Royal West Kents' camp at Fort Horstead, Chatham. When I went home for a weekend's leave, I wasn't well again. My mother called in the family doctor who said that I wasn't fit to travel back to Chatham.

After a wait of a few days, an ambulance came from the Barrack Hospital at Maidstone and picked me up. I stayed in the Hospital over Christmas and into January. I was then sent to the Military Hospital at Chatham and then to the Voluntary Aid Detachment Hospital at Seal, near Sevenoaks. This latter Hospital was owned by Lord Hillingdon. After a stay there I was returned to the Chatham Hospital where the doctors came to the conclusion that I would never be fit enough to be able to go to the front again.

On the afternoon of George's Day, April 23rd, I drew a civvy suit, an overcoat, a tie and a cap: the rest; boots, socks and underwear, I already had. So on the afternoon of April 24^{th,} 1918, I once more became a civilian and was given a railway warrant to take me as far as Wrotham Station. From there I went home to my parents and Ethel, who was now helping them with the work on the small holding.

Ethel didn't waste any time, and the next day she went to see the Rector of Plaxtol Church, the Reverend Wilmot Phillips. She arranged for our marriage for ten days later on May 4^{th,} 1918. My brother Fred was already back home as he was recovering from the injuries that he had received when that Whizz Bang went off. Part of his left knee had been shattered, and he now was only able to walk with the help of a walking stick. Oh, weren't the both of us so lucky to have got home alive, when so many others had lost their lives in those terrible battles of 1915 and 1916. Fred lived to his sixtieth year when he had a heart attack and died peacefully, sitting in his chair beside his fireside.

I began to remember now what that medical officer at the Casualty Clearing Station said to me in France.

He had said: 'You will never go back to the trenches and it will be a long, long time before you will be fit again.'

How true his words were. While I was in hospital in Maidstone, a specialist on tropical diseases asked me if I could remember ever following troops into billets or tents. When I thought back, I remembered once following some Sikh soldiers into some tents, and I slept on the ground as they had done. This doctor said that it was probably lice from them, which had the malaria germ that crawled on to my body and gave the disease to me. I have also often wondered whether it could have been from the Indian Orderly at the Casualty Clearing Station. He had dressed my open wounds on my leg after the boils had been lanced. The fever stayed with me for many years and even now still occurs at times. Even now, at times, my vest gets very yellow, especially when the sun gets very hot. But again all that happened is part of my survival story and how I am a survivor of that terrible war.

Well, the morning of May 4th started off with Scottish Mist falling, although the day soon turned beautiful and sunny. My brother and I had about two and a half miles to walk to Plaxtol Church. It was forbidden to hire taxis because of the fuel shortage, and we didn't fancy riding bicycles in our good clothes. The only exception to the taxi rule was a funeral. There were very few private cars on the roads in those days. Well, we started off giving ourselves loads of time to get to the Church for the wedding which was scheduled for 2.00pm. There was Fred limping along with the aid of a stick, and me, pretty nearly exhausted by the time that we reached the church. Fortunately, we had plenty of time to sit and recover in the cool of the inside of the church.

As the church clock was striking 2.00pm, the door opened, and my dear Ethel came in on the arm of her father, with her sisters, Florence, Queenie, Nellie, Hilda and Bessie following behind. Ethel had made her own dress from a dove grey material, and it was magnificent. She also wore a pretty floral hat, but it was the lovely smile on her dear face that will always remain with me as long as I live.

Well, the service was just a very simple marriage ceremony, and after we had settled with the Rector, he gave us a special blessing. He had known Ethel and her sisters since they were small. We then started to walk back to Ethel's parents' home which was thankfully much nearer than my parents' home. I was feeling on top of the world.

We walked back to Bourne Farm where her Dad had worked as a Bailiff for many years and Oh what a surprise we had. The Baker had made a white loaf for our wedding tea. You see, for a long time now there had been a shortage of flour and people in Britain had been having bread made of other things as well as wheat. The bread hadn't been very nice to eat. This lovely white loaf was a joy to behold and made the meal very special. Ethel and I stayed with my parents for a little while after our marriage and then she was given the key of a cottage which had become vacant and which was owned by Mr Harry Wolfe, a friend of her parents.

So now we had a four bedroomed cottage for which we paid four shillings a week rent. Our honeymoon started when we moved in and went on for the next fifty-two years when my darling left me and passed on in May 1970. Never in all those fifty-two years did we ever quarrel, or wish the other one dead as so many people seem to say today. I always said, and continue to say to this day, that if Ethel hadn't been waiting for me after those four terrible years; I would never have survived as many years as I have, which is now eighty-two years. It was her kindness and her loving devotion in the first ten years of our marriage that helped me to gradually regain my health and be able to work once more. For that love and devotion, I now say, as I always said to you my darling, thank you from the bottom of my heart. And may God have taken you to himself and peace in Heaven.

EPILOGUE

When I gave a commitment to my Grandfather that I would try and understand what the front line soldiers must have gone through in World War One, I wasn't in possession of the manuscript written by Sid Kemp. I was very upset at how so many of those who set off for France in 1914 should have died on the various battlefields, and that was my motivation in writing this book.

The biggest problem that I faced in tackling this subject was that I would channel the research I would have to carry out in a way that would support my opinions. I would then have great difficulty giving an accurate explanation of what actually happened and who was to blame. Obtaining Sid's manuscript setting out his personal experiences made my task a lot simpler as I can let him tell his story and you, the reader, can be the judge and jury.

I have tried to keep my own views out of it, and my reflections are mostly based on what Sid wrote about his day to day experiences which were affected by the events that he participated in.

The title I have chosen for the book reflects a commonly held belief which I wholeheartedly agree with. The British and Commonwealth 'Tommy' was a fine soldier and was worthy of the label of being a 'Lion'. I have found nothing in what Sid has written to change my opinion that the Generals, or most of them, were 'Donkeys'.

It is possible to say that Field Marshal Haig was right in his tactic that if we killed more Germans than they killed allied troops, then we would win the war. In my mind that makes the strategy in which the war was conducted by the Generals as even more pathetic. I don't agree that Haig had a mandate from the British Public to use the tactic of attrition. Some of the Generals who were on his staff were able to mount offensives successfully without massive losses. I have already referred you to Monash and what he was able to achieve. One of the significant advantages that Monash had was that he was an Australian and he was able to organise political pressure during the times when he was threatened with being overruled and sacked. If he was ordered to attack when he knew that his troops and other aspects of the offensive weren't ready, he said NO. He was thankfully a tough cookie.

Sid tells us that during one offensive they ran out of hand grenades and they had to give up hard earned gains because of the shortage. During another offensive, the artillery were on an allocation of three shells per gun per day. Surely it would have been simple to draw up ground rules that would have to be complied with before an attack was launched? I am sure that all you who have read Sid's account would be able to do a pretty good job of making a stab at a list of essentials.

When you read about the Battle of Loos or the Battle of the Somme you can pick out very accurate casualty figures - July 1st, 1916, 20,000 casualties. If you go to the cemeteries, you can read the names of those who were killed. The casualty figures are made up of individual deaths, and each one of these had a present, plus a past with parents, wives, brothers, sisters, etc., back in England, Scotland, Wales, Newfoundland, Australia and many other countries. The Commanders didn't know the individuals they were sending to their certain death; they were just a statistic to them. If there was a slight improvement in the casualty rate they felt that their strategies were working better; what they forgot was that even one man lost was somebody's family destroyed.

Obviously, in a war, the front line soldier is at great risk of being killed. That is what war is about, and there is no criticism if casualties are within justifiable limits. What is totally unacceptable is that men are sacrificed due to incompetency. What Sid has shown in his account is that there was a huge lack of a professional approach by the Generals. In fact, only for the agility and bravery of the troops in the trenches and their willingness to obey orders, even when they knew they were being asked to do crazy things; the war would have been lost.

DEDICATION

This book is dedicated to the memory of Sid Kemp who kept a diary while he was serving with the Queens Own Royal West Kent Regiment from the time he enlisted in August 1914 until he was invalided out of the Army in 1917. The Diary is what he used to write his account. I would have loved to have known the man as it is easy to pick out his qualities through the way he describes his experiences. He was definitely a man of integrity.

The book is also dedicated to his Brother Fred and all those who enlisted with him but never returned to England as they were killed in that dreadful war. We owe them all a great deal of gratitude.

I would also like to dedicate it to my Grandfather Lieutenant Colonel H.T.Cantan CMG of the Duke of Cornwall's Light Infantry who lost his life in 1916 at Arras.

Ray Cantan also writes over the name

PATRICK SLANEY

Historical Romance
The Smiles and Tears of Love

Family/War
War Brothers
The Tirpitz Legacy

Vince Hamilton Crime Mysteries
The Diamond Chain
Curse of Thieves
Danger Down Under
An African Adventure

These books are all available from Amazon in book or electronic format.